Women
and Womanhood
in America

PROBLEMS IN
AMERICAN CIVILIZATION

Under the editorial direction of
Edwin C. Rozwenc
Amherst College

Women and Womanhood in America

Edited and with an introduction by
Ronald W. Hogeland
University of Wisconsin at Stevens Point

With a foreword by
Aileen S. Kraditor
Boston University

D.C. HEATH AND COMPANY
Lexington, Massachusetts Toronto London

Published simultaneously in Canada.

Printed in the United States of America.

International Standard Book Number: 0-669-85597-9

Library of Congress Catalog Card Number: 73-6194

FOREWORD

It is currently fashionable in some scholarly circles to contend that worthwhile work in the histories of oppressed groups can be done only by members of those groups. Whites cannot write black history; men cannot write women's history. The logic of this assertion would lead to the conclusion that living people cannot write the history of dead people—that is, any history—for all historiography requires a capacity for empathy, for seeing the world through the eyes of people who were molded by social experiences different from the historian's own, precisely the capacity that this popular notion implicitly denies to all historians whatever their subject.

Certainly there is a special type of empathy that a member of the group under study can bring to the task of writing its history, despite the ever-present temptation to assume a greater similarity of experiences than actually exists and to evaluate the past by criteria that have meaning only in the present. Yet all professionals in the field of American history are aware of the special insights made possible by the foreign perspective of the English historians W. R. Brock and J. R. Pole; Americans' understanding of their government and politics was enormously enriched by Lord Bryce; the list is endless. Such contributions were made possible by the mixture of involvement and detachment, of empathy and perspective, that is occasionally found in a perceptive outsider. I would even contend that total identification is as great an impediment to productive scholarship as is total detachment—that a black historian who cannot empathize with the white oppressors is cut off from certain insights into the relations between blacks and whites, and that a woman historian incapable of entering into the minds of antifeminist men and women in the period she is studying is thereby cut off from understanding crucial aspects of women's history.

I have seen criticisms of certain male historians' books on women's history that express indignation that a man should presume to write in this field. The fallacy in this attitude is so obvious that its acceptance can be explained only by the particular stage that the new feminism is going through. The sudden discovery by women, including women historians, that they have grievances of which they had been only half-conscious, that they *can* speak openly of them, that they *can* write the history of their half of the human race, has been a liberating event. But, along with pride and the determination to correct historical distortions, it has in some instances released bitterness, once suppressed or diverted into other channels, and the overt hostility that always characterizes oppressed groups that see freedom ahead. Such feelings are understandable, but they do not provide a valid basis for criticism of a historical work. If a male historian writes women's history badly, it should be criticized as bad history. The same criticism of course should be made of women's or other history written badly by a woman. The standards for both should be the same: factual correctness, adequacy of evidence, coherence of hypothesis, the degree to which the work increases our understanding of the subject, and so on.

Rather than being resentful of the work of those male historians who are, in increasing numbers, specializing in women's studies, women should be delighted. When in the past was this a respectable field for male scholars? The objections to their "presumption" are exactly paralleled by the pressure that is being exerted on some women historians to specialize in women's studies even when their particular interests lie elsewhere, a pressure that in effect denies them the same freedom as men to choose their fields of study according to their individual talents and interests and personality bents; it is a scholarly form of the dictum that a woman's place is in the home—that is, with "women's" concerns.

All the above considerations lead me to rejoice when I see an anthology such as this one, the work of a scholar with a real "feel" for the subject, who has read widely in it and thought deeply about it, who has compiled a group of documents that take the reader step by step through the implications of a leading theme with thoughtful comments along the way—and who just happens to be a man.

Aileen S. Kraditor
Boston University

CONTENTS

III NINETEENTH-CENTURY AMERICA

Contemporary Observations

Commentary

IV TWENTIETH-CENTURY AMERICAN LIFE

Conflicting Opinions

Critique

INTRODUCTION

The purpose of this volume is threefold. First, its broadest design is to introduce the reader to a historical discussion of the nature of womanhood and the role women have played throughout the American experience. As a by-product of this aim the book is intended as a corrective to the notion held by many historians that, because women have been divorced from power, they are not worth writing about. As the first two selections, by Aileen S. Kraditor and Gerda Lerner, illustrate, the fact that women have received little attention in our history books tells us more about the historian's priorities than it does about female Americans. That is, since the search to recapture America's past has been almost exclusively a male preoccupation, it is not accidental that historical scholarship has focused upon such exclusively "masculine" topics as politics, economics and diplomacy.

Although this disposition has been challenged during the past half century with the advent and growth of social history (as well as disputed by the persistent dissent of the feminists), our understanding of the American woman has improved little. When women have appeared in history textbooks, all too often they are either reduced to a component of household management and childbearing, or are singled out because of their unconventional attitude and behavior. Ironically, the latter stereotype has been unwittingly perpetuated by the disproportionate attention given by some historians to the advocates of women's suffrage such as Elizabeth Cady Stanton and Susan B. Anthony. In any case, the effect of both approaches is similar. To write history as if women were not fully persons, or to picture them unintentionally as superhuman, is to reinforce the conventional disposition not to take female Americans seriously in pursuing historical truth. It is therefore the intention of the following selections to demonstrate that women as persons have had the capacity for a full range of human experience in the American past as well as to recognize their individual and collective contribution to American history.

Given this thrust, the subject of feminism has been subordinated to the larger story of the American woman. Characteristic of my approach is the inclusion of Ann Stanford's essay about the ambivalent revisionist, Anne Bradstreet, instead of a selection devoted to the more popular story of the radical, Anne Hutchinson. Secondly, the volume is designed to acquaint the student with some of the most recent scholarship in the field of women's studies. Although the table of contents indicates an equal number of primary and secondary sources, the latter selections constitute two-thirds of the reading material. This is essential for coming to terms with our subject since there has been almost no attempt to make a collection of scholarly materials available to the undergraduate. In contrast, a variety of readings in primary sources has become accessible by means of anthologies which usually focus on some aspect of the historical quest for women's rights.*

All of the subsequent secondary selections have been written in the last ten years. This is no accident. It underscores the fact that only recently have historians given this field of inquiry much serious consideration. Yet one should not equate the newness of the enterprise with a lack of maturity or creativity. To the contrary, the scholarship is substantial. Although the range of topics is still limited, the selections amply illustrate the marked, sophisticated advance made since Mary R. Beard and Sidney Ditzion wrote their important, but now prosaic, books, *Woman as Force in History* (1946), and *Marriage, Morals, and Sex in America* (1953).

The material was selected for its degree of excellence, its variety of subject matter and its type of approach. The initial selections by Aileen Kraditor and Gerda Lerner sound the keynote for the latter consideration. The essays by Winthrop D. Jordon, Walter O'Meara and Gerda Lerner are in part an attempt to give exposure to "minority women"—black, Indian and working women. The tenor of the

---

* An exception is Nancy F. Cott's *Root of Bitterness: Documents in the Social History of American Women* (New York, 1972), which does not limit itself to the women's rights movement.

scholarly articles reflects an indebtedness to the interdisciplinary approach in general and to the field of the history of social ideas in particular. Not only are other disciplinary methods employed such as literary criticism and psychology, but three essays are written by nonhistorians including a poet (Ann Stanford) and a sociologist (Alice S. Rossi). The summary of sources at the end of each essay is provided in order to give the student a sense of other available scholarship.

Finally, the purpose of this collection of essays is to suggest to the reader that it is important to reach beyond women's history per se into the larger context of social relationships in order to fully come to terms with the subject of women and womanhood. That is, the study of the American woman should lead inevitably to a consideration of the role men and (male) conventional wisdom have played in determining the dimensions of "femininity" and what functions women were able to have in society. In turn this should tell us something about the nature of American manhood. Aileen Kraditor in her introductory essay explores this dynamic, and many of the subsequent secondary readings develop the theme. In addition, I have attempted to illustrate how conventional wisdom works by including a number of observations about womanhood by contemporary *non*reformers (both male and female).

Hence, the volume's design is to augment the student's understanding of woman's accomplishments in American life and her status in any given historical period by emphasizing male-female relationships within the context of social ideas. To this extent its intent is somewhat akin to that of "racial history" compared to black studies or Negro history. My disposition here is not to minimize the vitality that women's history has demonstrated, nor negate its contribution to our collective wisdom. Rather it is to reaffirm the necessity to integrate the study of women into the larger contours of human consciousness and experience.

I APPROACHES TO STUDYING WOMEN IN AMERICAN HISTORY

The essays in this introductory part provide the reader with two distinct approaches to the subject of women in American history. This is not to say, however, that Professors Kraditor and Lerner have no viewpoints in common. They do. For example, both agree that the subject has been neglected by historians; both believe that it should be approached in a scholarly manner; and both are aware of the fact that, historically, women have had limited opportunities in the areas of economics, education and politics. Most importantly, both historians maintain the study of women in American history is at the "take-off" stage of development and that, while informative studies will always be needed, primary attention should now be shifted toward interpretive analysis.

Yet they do differ significantly. Admittedly Professor Kraditor's essay focuses on the history of feminism and Lerner's on the general topic of women's history, but there is more at stake than this. Central to Kraditor's approach is her awareness that one can not deal adequately with the subject of women or womanhood without seriously considering the forces that have shaped their experience. The student of women's history must attempt to relate women to the "climate of opinion" in which they lived. A consideration of feminism and antifeminism is one avenue of tracing the historical struggle of women for self-determination. Indeed, the author's emphasis on the quest for "autonomy"—to be regarded as people rather than as the female relatives of people—can be applied as well to the social and personal experience of women. The implication of Kraditor's approach is clear: to apply a "separate but equal" conceptual framework to the study of women in American history is to perpetuate the notion that female Americans are inferior and not worth talking about.

1

In contrast, Professor Lerner gives priority to restoring the record of women's achievements in American life in such areas as the development of the frontier, reform movements, and daily economic life. In order to accomplish this task successfully, she argues, historians must be willing to judge women's contributions differently from men's. This is to say, since women's role in society has been unlike their male counterparts, "their achievements must be measured on a different scale," yet still equal in importance. Lerner's recently published survey, The Woman in American History (1971), well illustrates this approach by dealing almost exclusively with prominent women/movements and their related accomplishments.

Aileen S. Kraditor

UP FROM THE PEDESTAL

Professor Kraditor (b. 1928) teaches at Boston University and is the author of The Ideas of the Woman Suffrage Movement *(1965); and* Means and Ends in American Abolitionism *(1969).*

Women in History and Historiography

Until toward the end of the nineteenth century, most history was written in terms of kings' reigns and presidents' administrations, of wars and revolutions; in these, women took little or no part. And, since women wrote as little history as they made, it is not surprising that historiography faithfully reflected their exclusion from those events historians considered important enough to record. That their exclusion was itself a datum of history never entered the historians' minds, for was not the domestic sphere—ahistorical by definition— "naturally" ordained to be woman's? "Natural" phenomena—geographical, meteorological, astronomical, ecological, and so on—are noticed by the historian only when they intrude in a positive—i.e., *un*natural—way in the human drama; ordinarily they are simply "there," negative, the stage on which the drama takes place. Hence the older histories sometimes opened with a chapter setting the geographical stage and often included narrative-breaking chapters on social life, family patterns, dress styles, and other such entertaining topics that changed either too slowly or too fast to be part of the mainstream of "real" history. It is hardly coincidental that such chapters, which of course mentioned women, performed a function in these tomes parallel to that of comic interludes in Shakespeare's tragedies. Until a few years ago this situation had continued with little noticeable change.

In 1946 Mary Beard noted that twenty-two years earlier Arthur M. Schlesinger had called for a rewriting of American history to give proper credit to the role women had played in it. She complained that his suggestion had gone unheeded, and observed that Ralph Gabriel, in his *Course of American Democratic Thought,* published in 1940, had completely ignored even the woman's-rights movement.[1] The seventy-year struggle for woman suffrage had evidently contributed nothing to the course of American democratic thought. In 1968 Schlesinger's complaint of 1922 and Mrs. Beard's of 1946 are still timely: the index of a widely used college text in United States history lists only forty-nine women, and their segregation into special sections is made more invidious by the fact that these individuals or women in general are mentioned on only 4.1 percent of the work's 1,600 pages.[2] But there are signs that no historian in 1990 will have occasion to quote three such complaints, each a generation later than the one before, and add a fourth. Two major facts provide grounds for optimism: first, the entrance of women into those areas of American life that traditionally furnished the data of history, and, second, the rise to popularity of social history and the growing tendency of even the political, constitutional, diplomatic, and economic historians to incorporate data of social history in their studies. The history of women's role and women's status may follow the pattern of Negro history: before World War II it was largely ignored except by Negro scholars; since then it has become an important area of specialization and will continue to be until the enormous gaps in our knowledge begin to narrow. A third stage, heralded by a recent article,[3] will begin when Negro history is incorporated into all other aspects of American history, as scholars both recognize the integral role of Negroes in American life from the beginning and possess sufficient specialized studies to perform the synthesis. The history of women is at the beginning of the second stage of this process.

Until a few years ago, scholarly works on the role and status of women in American history fell into two categories. The first consisted of only two books—Eleanor Flexner's *Century of Struggle* (Cambridge, Mass., 1959) and Andrew Sinclair's *The Better Half* (New York, 1965)—both broad surveys and both about as good as the paucity of the specialized knowledge at their disposal allowed.

[1] Mary R. Beard, *Woman as Force in History: A Study in Traditions and Realities* (New York, 1946), pp. 58–59; Arthur M. Schlesinger, *New Viewpoints in American History* (New York, 1922); Ralph H. Gabriel, *The Course of American Democratic Thought: An Intellectual History Since 1815* (New York, 1940).
[2] Harry J. Carman, Harold C. Syrett, and Bernard W. Wishy, *A History of the American People,* 2 vols., paperback (3rd ed., New York, 1967). The title is ironic.
[3] Robert Starobin, "The Negro: A Central Theme in American History," *Journal of Contemporary History,* III (April 1968), 37–53.

By far the majority of works in this field fell into the second category: biographies of important women and minute accounts of activities of suffragists in various states.

The biographical approach is not by accident the most popular; nor is it accidental that almost all these works are by women. Most men, even today, when women are legally almost their equal, think of the woman's-rights movement as the demand by neurotic females to be like men, and they assume that a significant proportion of its members were hawk-faced spinsters who wore blue stockings and marched in parades for lack of more feminine employments to occupy them. (It may be more than a coincidence that most male historians, when they do mention the suffragists, call them "suffragettes," the epithet that during the life of the movement was used only by their enemies.) With a few exceptions, only women have seen fit to write about the lives of women leaders, and these biographies, while they give the lie to the stereotype, are rarely accorded by male historians a respectable place in historical literature and are hardly ever mentioned in bibliographies appended to books that deal with the times in which these women affected history. Hence women scholars who can be expected to harbor a better opinion of their sex have had the field to themselves. But even they have not been fully immune to the dominant ideological assumptions. This accounts in part for their biographical approach, which manifests a concentration of attention on and interest in the personal motivations of leading participants in the movement and a corresponding slighting of the objective historical significance of the movement in the mainstream of American history. Moreover, the biographical approach results partly from their desire to demonstrate the normality of their subjects; this laudable aim unfortunately has resulted in some portrayals that are larger than lifesize and hence smaller than reality.

The articles on suffragist activity hardly deserve the name of history. They are, rather, the raw material for history, meticulously gathered from private papers, newspapers, state legislative documents, and the like. They list names and dates in bewildering profusion. They tell which lady gave a tea party for suffragists on which afternoon in which town, how much money was raised, and which local paper recorded the event. They tell little about why these women wanted the vote or why the movement arose where and when it did. . . .

. . . The informative studies of women continue to be needed, but they do not themselves suggest how they will be integrated into larger explanatory patterns. This depends on a new attitude, on the part of historians, toward women and toward the relation of social history to other aspects of history. Already young male scholars are devoting serious attention to this field, and a few scholars, such as William R. Taylor,[4] are considering women's roles and status as part of the necessary data for intellectual history. The requisite shift in attitude can be described by means of a phrase that American feminists repeatedly used in their propaganda: a change from regarding women as females who happen to be human, to regarding them as humans who happen to be female. For, as long as the first attitude prevailed, it was logical to omit women from accounts of the lives and activities of human beings—that is, from history—and to mention them for the same reason that other nonhistorical phenomena were mentioned, as part of the "natural" setting against which the human drama was enacted. In view of the primitive state of historiography in this field, the larger explanatory patterns suggested in the following pages can be no more than tentative.

Feminism and Antifeminism: The Real Issues

Feminism is customarily thought of as the theory that women should have political, economic, and social rights equal to those of men. As a definition of a theory, this is satisfactory, but a theory has a way of changing when it is translated into practice over a long period of time. At times some of the feminists whose writings are sampled in this book demanded social rights superior to those of men; at other times, political, economic, and social rights inferior to those of men but superior to those that women had; and at still other times, rights different from but "equal" to those of men. In one period the most commonly demanded right was higher education; in another, access to professions; in a third, the vote. Clearly, the history of American feminism implies far more than the practical application of the theory stated above—that women should have rights equal to men's. What the feminists have wanted has added up to something more fundamental than any specific set of rights or the sum total of all the rights that men have had.

[4] *Cavalier and Yankee: The Old South and the National Character* (London, 1963).

This fundamental something can perhaps be designated by the term "autonomy." Whether a feminist's demand has been for all the rights men have had, or for some but not all of the rights men have had, or for certain rights that men have not had, the grievance behind the demand has always seemed to be that women have been regarded not as people but as female relatives of people. And the feminists' desire has, consequently, been for women to be recognized, in the economic, political, and/or social realms, as individuals in their own right. Such a recognition could be consistent with a distinction between men's and women's "spheres," even with a continued subordination of the feminine "sphere," as well as with a merging of men's and women's "spheres." The essential change demanded has always been that women's "sphere" must be defined by women. The questions have always been: What is women's proper sphere? and, even more, Who should decide what that sphere is? . . .

The suggestion that autonomy, rather than the redefinition of women's proper sphere, should be considered the objective toward which the feminists, consciously or unconsciously, worked is not meant to deny the importance of the question of "spheres." Rather, it is meant to show that that question has broader implications than commonly thought. The feminists seemed to sense that the distance between the spheres of men and women encouraged people to lose sight of the differences among individual women. Strictly speaking, men have never had a "proper sphere," since their sphere has been the world and all its activities. They have always been, accordingly, human beings who happened to be male. Women, on the contrary, have occupied sharply circumscribed spheres—the home, the church, the philanthropic society or sewing circle—regardless of differences among individuals in talents and tastes, and have, accordingly, been thought of as females who happened to be human. It has been taken for granted that men's activities should vary according to their potentialities, but it has been assumed that women's activities should be defined by their sex. Thus, it was proper for men to live for themselves—to achieve self-fulfillment by developing their individual talents—whereas women should live for others—to achieve self-fulfillment by caring for their husbands and children. Church and charity work was a logical extension of that role outside the home and hence was socially acceptable.

Women have been the only subordinated group that has belonged to the same families as its rulers. The ambiguous status of well-to-do women, as both ruler and ruled, generated contradictions and ambiguities in both feminists' and antifeminists' attitudes toward women. On the one hand, the middle-class women who in the nineteenth century comprised the feminist movement shared the economic and social status of their men, but, on the other, they were excluded from the economic functions that maintained that status. While they shared the middle-class ideology, on all issues besides feminism, that rationalized their status, their desire for individual autonomy seemed to conflict with that ideology's understanding of the nature of the family and its relation to society. The feminist movement began in the middle of the nineteenth century, when both individualism and the cult of domesticity occupied extremely important places in American popular thought. Two such contrary doctrines could co-exist only if individualism was marked "For Men Only." The glorification of the Jacksonian go-getter businessman, the intrepid pioneer, the log-cabin-born President, coincided with the decline in women's status and the increasing restriction of middle-class women to domestic and ornamental functions. . . .

Just as the specific content of the feminists' demands expressed a deeper and broader urge for self-determination in general, the specific content of their opponents' conservatism on the woman question reflected their attitude toward American society in general. Certain recurrent themes in antifeminist literature portray the business and political world as one of strife, and the home as a peaceful refuge, where the higher values are nourished. The ugly features of the outside world are accepted as necessary for progress, but progress would be futile unless balanced and ennobled by the conservative influence of the home. Destruction of the home means destruction of the delicate balance between progress and stability, between warfare and peace, between a certain necessary brutality and an equally necessary refinement. How might the home be destroyed? By eradicating the distinction between the spheres of men and women. If women enter the political and business world, they will become like men—or rather, owing to their inherently emotional nature, become even more brutal and coarse than men. Thus, not all antifeminists contended that women were inferior to men; in fact, a few conceded that women could vote as intelligently, conduct businesses as shrewdly, or engage in scholarly pursuits as creatively as men. But what price would society pay for these additional voters, merchants, and scholars? Social disorder. The home was the bulwark against social disorder, and woman was the creator of the home. Not all nineteenth-century antifeminists were insincere when they sang poetic praises to the Queen of the Household, who was superior to the man even though she was excluded from the polls and professions. In their curiously ambiguous conception of American society—a conception that glorified its quick change and yet feared the consequences of that change—she occupied a desperately necessary place as symbol and center of the one institution that prevented society from flying apart. Hence the apparent contradiction of a society increasingly seen as a conglomerate of separate individuals which nevertheless insisted on assigning a "sphere" to half its population according not to their individual but to their common characteristics, and insisting that the unit of representation in the state was not the individual but the family. And hence the apparent anomaly of antifeminist tracts antedating the rise of the feminist movement. If antifeminism is understood as largely representing fear of social disorder, the contradiction and the anomaly disappear. It was not that social order required the subordination of women; rather, to the conservatives it required a *family structure* that involved the subordination of women.

Aspects of the History of American Feminism

. . . A deeper look at the antebellum generation . . . suggests that the Industrial Revolution was the soil in which feminism grew. The influence was indirect, for the women exploited in the new factories were not those who became feminists; in fact, feminist propaganda rarely mentioned women's wages and conditions in industrial enterprises until about the turn of the century, when the woman's-rights movement was half a century old. And it is difficult to attribute a direct influence to the congestion of population in cities and the tendency of families to become smaller, both consequences of industrialism; many of the early feminists were small-town residents with large broods. In any case, these processes might make a feminist movement possible; they would not cause its development.

On the other hand, the growth of industry made the United States a magnet for Irish immigration in the forties, providing middle-class women with abundant domestic help, which in turn gave them leisure for self-education and reform activities. (The reform movements themselves can be seen as reactions to the social problems created by rapid economic development.) Women whose horizons had been thus broadened and who wished to enlarge their sphere of activity then encountered the prejudice against such activity that lit the first spark of feminism. The growth of industry also broadened the distinctions between men's and women's occupations and certainly provoked new thinking about the significance and permanence of their respective "spheres."[5] The rise in the urban population resulted in the enfranchisement of all white men and consequently in the belief that a man earned the vote by his membership in the human race rather than by his ownership of property; a woman who considered herself a member of the human race might question the justice of her disfranchisement. Most important of all, perhaps, was the rapid social change caused ultimately by the rise of industry. The feminist movement may, then, be best characterized as an effect of various effects of the Industrial Revolution.

Throughout its history American feminism has been overwhelmingly a white, middle-class movement. This does not mean that Negro and working-class women have not wanted equality of the sexes. They have formed their own organizations (demanding, among other things, woman suffrage), and have in small numbers belonged to various feminist organizations. One reason for the minor part they have played in them has been the obvious prejudice against them within the woman's-rights movement. Far more important has been their own sense of priorities. Whereas middle-class women wanted the same freedom to develop individual talents as their men apparently had, black and working-class women knew that these things were denied *them* not primarily because they were women but because they belonged to groups whose male members were denied them as well. The demand for woman suffrage necessarily seemed less important than the demand for security of person or for a living

[5] For a full discussion of the impact of the Industrial Revolution on women's status and the rise of feminism, see Keith E. Melder, "The Beginnings of the Women's Rights Movement in the United States, 1800–1840," Ph.D. dissertation, Yale, 1964. Some of the points mentioned above are in Melder, Preface and chap. 1.

wage, and the request for admission to colleges had to appear irrelevant to a mother whose children left school to work in factory or field. Hence Negro and working-class women have always put their needs and grievances as Negroes and workers first and as women second. Primary emphasis on feminism seems to have been a luxury that only white, middle-class women have been able to afford.

In the face of the nineteenth-century assumption that men and women differed innately in mental, moral, and personality traits, the feminists undertook a formidable task when they challenged the notion of separate "spheres" and demanded autonomy for women as individuals. Even those who agreed that woman's place was in the home had to demonstrate that homemakers could also be professionals, voters, and businesswomen. But until the late nineteenth century there were few such women they could point to as living proofs of their contention, and they had to admit that a much larger proportion of women than of men were politically naïve, emotional, uncreative mechanically and artistically, slavish followers of fashion, and interested in little beyond their homes and families. Since the feminists' demand for autonomy could not be justified by much empirical evidence and indeed seemed to contradict the evidence, they at first adopted two main tactics that permitted them to ignore or even admit unpleasant facts: they appealed to abstract justice and they insisted that these "feminine" traits were not innate but the results of training. . . .

The contention that only when women had the opportunity to discover all their aptitudes could their proper sphere be defined appeared regularly in feminist propaganda from its first appearance to our own day. Feminists have at the same time been eager to show that this or that particular career was appropriate for women, and so the demand for education was only the first of many demands for specific rights. They included the right to become physicians, to go to college, to practice law, to be the legal guardians of their children, and so on. Propaganda along these lines had a double function: first, it was a plea for a wider range of opportunities; second, it exploited every bit of evidence it could uncover to prove that women had already demonstrated the qualifications for fulfilling these roles, perhaps as much to instill self-confidence in women as to show that women's talents were as varied as men's. . . .

The Family vs. Autonomy

The years since the enactment of the Nineteenth Amendment have
seen the publication of countless essays explaining modern American woman's discontent with the results of suffrage and of the large
measure of freedom she has won. Many of these bear a remarkable
resemblance to very early antifeminist tracts in their contention that
woman is after all destined to be fulltime wife, mother, and home-
maker. Betty Friedan's *Feminine Mystique* documents the fact that
these ideas are winning increasing acceptance among young women
themselves.

If the "autonomy" thesis is correct, perhaps the discontent is due
not to disappointment with the results of the attainment of equality,
but to the discovery that the array of specific, formal rights has not
added up to substantive equality and autonomy. Although many discriminatory laws still exist in many states, they are minor and hardly
touch the lives of most women. Yet the old grievance remains:
women are still, in popular thought and custom, females first and
human beings second. Is this merely an instance of "cultural lag"?
Or is it that the persistence of the old attitude reflects the persistence
of the institution of the family in essentially the same form it had when
the feminist movement first arose?

Many tracts written between the Civil War and World War I either
called for or predicted the mechanization and professionalization of
homemaking chores. They noted that all other varieties of necessary
labor had become social, had been made efficient through division
of labor, had become the work of paid experts. Yet housework remained the job of untrained isolated women. They assumed that once
middle-class women had won the right to work beyond the domestic
sphere they would automatically do so, if only they could be freed
from household drudgery. . . .

The frequency of such predictions cannot be a coincidence. Obviously the inferior position of women was somehow associated with
the isolation of each family from every other family and with the
sex-determined division of labor within the family. Yet the predictions have not been fulfilled. A century ago the sexual division of
labor within the middle-class family could be justified by the fact
that housekeeping (even with the help of a maid) was a time-consuming job. But in our day cause and effect seem to have been

reversed: the conviction that the sexual division of labor within the home is "right" has now become an incentive to *make* housekeeping a fulltime job when technology has rendered it no longer necessary. And so we find women baking their own bread, making their children's clothes, and in other ways multiplying their household chores —enacting a sort of Parkinson's Law of housewifery.[6]

It is no longer possible for a middle-class feminist to argue that women are relegated to the domestic sphere by either law or the need of a wife to keep house while her husband works to support the family. In a period when there is no longer a rational basis for allocating either remunerative work or homemaking tasks according to sex, the institution of the family itself, as popularly conceived, stands revealed as the obstacle to full sex equality. As long as the man engages more in the work of the world and the woman spends a large proportion of her time and energies in the isolated family circle, men will continue to lead in government, the professions, and all the other fields that provide us with our criteria of human achievement. Some contend that women can use their education and talents (innately equal to men's) in training their children. But it may be argued that the training of children requires less than the highest level of specialization and provides no incentive and opportunity to push back the frontiers of knowledge. These must remain the province of men so long as women, regardless of their individual aptitudes, retain the principal responsibility of child care. And the current entrance of many men into the elementary-school teaching profession will help to discredit the assumption that child care is innately woman's work. It is also sometimes argued that women need not lament their lack of opportunity to specialize in given fields of knowledge; they can be the "generalists," reading in many more subjects than their specialist husbands have time to do. But such generalization ordinarily precludes that depth of mastery of one field that permits original and creative contributions to it; again, the pioneers and geniuses must be the men. A third common argument is that the difference in familial roles need not be synonymous with inequality: women will continue to be the nurturers and conservers, men the explorers and innovators, each's contribution to society equally necessary. It can be argued that this separate-but-equal doctrine

[6] See Betty Friedan, *The Feminine Mystique* (New York, 1963), chap. 10, "Housewifery Expands to Fill the Time Available."

disguises the fact that the roles of men and women, thus defined, perpetuate the ancient source of the feeling that women are inferior. Men's role as explorers and innovators places a premium on their individual talents, whereas women's role as nurturers and conservers actually places such talents at a discount.[7] This third argument, then, is a new way of stating an old myth: that men are male *humans* whereas women are human *females*. . . .

In short, inequality of the sexes still exists because the family structure has remained basically unchanged. Unless a middle-class feminist is prepared to challenge that family structure head-on, contemporary feminism will perhaps revert to the form of the earliest feminism—the generalized urge toward individual autonomy—before feminists concentrated their efforts on winning a long list of specific rights which they assumed would add up to autonomy.

[7] For a perceptive discussion of this problem, see Alice S. Rossi, "Barriers to the Career Choice of Engineering, Medicine, or Science among American Women," in Jacquelyn A. Mattfeld and Carol G. Van Aken, eds., *Women and the Scientific Professions: The M.I.T. Symposium on American Women in Science and Engineering* (Cambridge, Mass., 1965), pp. 51–127, esp. pp. 116–24. The article is of more generalized interest than its title suggests.

Gerda Lerner

NEW APPROACHES TO THE STUDY OF WOMEN IN AMERICAN HISTORY

Professor Lerner (b. 1920) of Sarah Lawrence College, like Professor Kraditor, received her doctorate from Columbia University in the 1960s. Her major area of interest is women's history, and she has published two important books, The Grimké Sisters from South Carolina: Rebels Against Slavery *(1967); and* Black Women in White America: A Documentary History *(1972).*

The striking fact about the historiography of women is the general neglect of the subject by historians. As long as historians held to the traditional view that only the transmission and exercise of power were worthy of their interest, women were of necessity ignored. There was little room in political, diplomatic, and military history for American women, who were, longer than any other single group in the population, outside the power structure. At best their relationship to power was implicit and peripheral and could easily be passed over as insignificant. With the rise of social history and increasing concern with groups out of power, women received some attention, but interest was focused mainly on their position in the family and on their social status.[1] The number of women featured in textbooks of American history remains astonishingly small to this day, as does the number of biographies and monographs by professional historians.

The literature concerning the role of women in American history is topically narrow, predominantly descriptive, and generally devoid of interpretation. Except for the feminist viewpoint, there seems to be no underlying conceptual framework.

Feminist writers, not trained historians, were the first to undertake a systematic attempt to approach the problem of women's role in American life and history. This took the forms of feminist tracts, theoretical approaches, and compilations of woman's "contribu-

© 1969 by Peter N. Stearns. Reprinted from the *Journal of Social History,* Vol. 3, No. 1, pp. 53–62, by permission of the editor.

[1] Cf. Arthur Schlesinger, Sr., *New Viewpoints in American History* (New York, 1922), chap. 6. For a contemporary historian's viewpoint, see David M. Potter, "American Women and the American Character," in *American History and Social Sciences,* ed. Edward N. Saveth (New York, 1964), pp. 427–428.

tions."[2] The early compilers attacked the subject with a missionary zeal designed, above all, to right wrong. Their tendency was to praise anything women had done as a "contribution" and to include any women who had gained the slighest public attention in their numerous lists.[3] Still, much positive work was done in simply recounting the history of the woman's rights movement and some of its forerunners and in discussing some of the women whose pioneering struggles opened opportunities to others. Feminist writers were hampered by a twofold bias. First, they shared the middle-class, nativist, moralistic approach of the Progressives and tended to censure out of existence anyone who did not fit into this pattern. Thus we find that women like Frances Wright and Ernestine Rose received little attention because they were considered too radical. "Premature feminists" such as the Grimké sisters, Maria Weston Chapman, and Lydia Maria Child are barely mentioned. The second bias of the feminists lies in their belief that the history of women is important only as representing the history of an oppressed group and its struggle against its oppressors.

This latter concept underlies the somewhat heroic, collectively authored *History of Woman Suffrage.* This work, probably because it represents an easily available though disorganized collection of primary sources, has had a pervasive influence on later historians. Following the lead and interpretation of the feminists, professional historians have been preoccupied with the woman's rights movement in its legal and political aspects. Modern historians, too, think that what is important to know about women is how they got the ballot.[4]

The only serious challenge to this conceptual framework was offered by Mary Beard in the form of a vigorous though often fuzzy

---

[2] The most important feminist tracts before the launching of the woman's rights movement are: Charles Brockden Brown, *Alcuin: A Dialogue* (Boston, 1798); Sarah M. Grinké, *Letters on the Equality of the Sexes and the Condition of Woman* (Boston, 1838); and Margaret Fuller, *Woman in the Nineteenth Century* (Boston, 1844). The publications of the feminist movement are too numerous to list here; a representative collection is incorporated in Elizabeth C. Stanton, Susan B. Anthony, and Matilda J. Gage, *History of Woman Suffrage* (6 vols.; New York, 1881–1922).

[3] Typical of the "compilers" are: Lydia M. Child, *History of the Condition of Women* (2 vols.; New York, 1835); Sarah J. Hale, *Woman's Record. . . .* (New York, 1853); Phebe A. Hanaford, *Daughters of America, or Women of the Century* (Augusta, Me., n.d.); and Frances E. Willard and Mary A. Livermore, *American Women* (New York, 1897).

[4] Cf. Eleanor Flexner, *Century of Struggle: The Woman's Rights Movement in the United States* (Cambridge, Mass., 1959); Aileen S. Kraditor, *The Ideas of the Woman Suffrage Movement* (New York, 1965).

polemic against feminists.[5] What is important about women, said Mary Beard, is not that they were an oppressed group—she denied that they ever were—but that they have made a continuous and impressive contribution to society throughout all of history. It is a contribution, however, which does not fit into the value system generally accepted by historians when they make decisions as to who is or is not important to history. Mary Beard undertook in several of her books to trace the positive achievements of women, their social role, and their contributions to community life. Her concepts are most successfully reflected in *The Rise of American Civilization,* which she coauthored with her husband Charles Beard. In it the position of women is treated throughout in an integrated way with great attention to the economic contributions made by women.[6] But the Beards's approach to the subject of women had little influence on the historical profession. Perhaps this was due to the fact that in the 1930s and 1940s both the general public and historians became somewhat disenchanted with the woman's-rights movement.

The winning of suffrage had made only a slight change in the actual status of women, and other factors—technological and economic changes, access to higher education, changing sexual mores —now loomed a great deal larger. The impact of Freudianism and psychology had made reformers in general somewhat suspect. Feminism was not infrequently treated with the same humorous condescension as that other successful failure: temperance.

Women have received serious attention from economic historians. There is a good deal of excellent literature dealing with the problem of women workers. Women as contributors to the economy from colonial times on, the laws affecting them, their wages and working conditions, and their struggle for protective legislation have been fully described.[7] Although female labor leaders have not generally

[5] *Woman as Force in History* (New York, 1946).
[6] Mary R. Beard, *America Through Women's Eyes* (New York, 1934), *On Understanding Women* (New York, 1931), and *Women's Work in Municipalities* (New York, 1915); Charles R. and Mary R. Beard, *The Rise of American Civilization* (New York, 1927).
[7] For the economic life of colonial women see: Elisabeth A. Dexter, *Colonial Women of Affairs: Women in Business and Professions in America before 1776* (Boston, 1931), and *Career Women of America: 1776–1840* (Francestown, N.H., 1950); Richard B. Morris, *Government and Labor in Early America* (New York, 1946); and Julia C. Spruill, *Women's Life and Work in the Southern Colonies* (Chapel Hill, 1938). For women's economic role in nineteenth- and twentieth-century America, see: Edith Abbott, *Women in Industry* (New York, 1918); J. B. Andrews and W. D. P. Bliss, *Report on Condition of Woman and Child Wage-Earners in the United States* (19

been given much attention, their activities are on record. Excellent collections of material pertaining to women at Radcliffe and Smith College are available but remain insufficiently explored.

Modern historians of the reform movements have done much to restore a sane balance to female achievement in reform; yet one still finds excluded from notice certain women who would have been included as a matter of course had they been men. Sophie Loeb, Grace Dodge, and Mary Anderson could be cited as examples.[8]

The historical literature on the family in America is quite scanty, but there seems to be a revival of interest in the subject. Several interesting monographs have begun to deal with the family role of women in its various aspects. This approach is promising and will hopefully be pursued by other historians.[9]

A new conceptual framework for dealing with the subject of women in American history is needed. The feminist frame of reference has become archaic and fairly useless. The twentieth-century revolution in technology, morality, education, and employment patterns has brought enormous changes in the status and role of American women; these changes demand a historical perspective and understanding. The emergence of a recent "new feminism" is a social phenomenon requiring interpretation. Most importantly, women themselves are as entitled as minority-group members are to having "their" history fully recorded.

Yet the subject is complex. It is difficult to conceptualize women as a group, since they are dispersed throughout the population. Except for special-interest organizations, they do not combine together. The subject is full of paradoxes which elude precise definitions and defy synthesis.

Women at various times and places were a majority of the population, yet their status was that of an oppressed minority, deprived of the rights men enjoyed. Women have for centuries been excluded

vols.; Doc. No. 645, 61st Congress, 2nd Session; Washington, 1910); and Elizabeth Baker, *Technology and Women's Work* (New York, 1964).

[8] For women in reform movements, see: Robert Bremmer, *American Philanthropy* (Chicago, 1960); Clarke E. Chambers, *Seedtime of Reform: American Social Service and Social Action, 1918–1933* (Ann Arbor, 1963); Christopher Lasch, *The New Radicalism in America: 1889–1963* (New York, 1965); and Daniel Levine, *Varieties of Reform Thought* (Madison, Wis., 1964).

[9] For a history of the family, see Arthur W. Calhoun, *A Social History of the American Family* (3 vols., Cleveland, 1918); Sidney Ditzion, *Marriage, Morals, and Sex in America* (New York, 1953); Paul H. Jacobson, *American Marriage and Divorce* (New York, 1959); and William O'Neill, *Divorce in the Progressive Era* (New Haven, 1967).

from positions of power, both political and economic, yet as members of families, as daughters and wives, they often were closer to actual power than many a man. If women were among the most exploited of workers, they were also among the exploiters. If some women were dissatisfied with their limited opportunities, most women were adjusted to their position in society and resisted efforts at changing it. Women generally played a conservative role as individuals and in their communities, the role of conserving tradition, law, order, and status quo. Yet women in their organizations were frequently allied with the most radical and even revolutionary causes and entered alliances with the very groups threatening the status quo.

If women themselves acted paradoxically, so did society in formulating its values for women. The rationale for women's peculiar position in society has always been that their function as mothers is essential to the survival of the group and that the home is the essential nucleus of society as we know it. Yet the millions of housewives and homemakers have throughout our history been deprived of the one tangible reward our society ranks highest: an income of their own. Neither custom, law, nor changes of technology, education, or politics have touched this sacred tradition. The unpaid housewife-and-mother has affected attitudes toward the women who perform homemaking services for strangers. Traditionally women in the service trades have been the lowest paid among all workers. Nor has this pattern been restricted to the unskilled groups. When women have entered an occupation in large numbers, this occupation has come to be regarded as low status and has been rewarded by low pay. Examples for this are readily found in the teaching and nursing fields. Even intellectual work has been treated with the same double standard. Creative fields in which women excel—poetry, the short story—have been those carrying the lowest rewards in money and esteem. Only in the performing arts has individual female talent had the same opportunity as male talent. Yet a cursory glance at the composition of any major symphony orchestra even today will reveal that in this field, too, opportunities for women have been restricted.

In dealing with the subject of women, studies frequently use other distinctive groups in our society as models for comparison. Women's position has variously been likened to that of the slaves, oppressed ethnic or racial minorities, or economically deprived groups. But these comparisons quickly prove inadequate. The slave comparison obviously was a rhetorical device rather than a factual statement even at the time when Harriet Martineau first made it.[10] While the law denied women equal citizenship and for certain purposes classed them with "Indians and imbeciles," it never denied them physical freedom nor did it regard them as "chattel personnel." In fact, even within the slavery system, women were oppressed differently from men. The "minority-group model" is also unsatisfactory. All members of a minority group which suffers discrimination share, with a very few exceptions, in the low-status position of the entire group. But women may be the wives of Cabinet members, the daughters of Congressmen, the sisters of business leaders, and yet seen simply as persons, they may be disfranchised and suffer from economic and educational discrimination. On the other hand, a lower-class woman may advance to a position of economic or social power simply by marriage, a route which is generally not open to members of racial minority groups. In one particular respect the minority-group comparison is illuminating: like Negroes, women suffer from "high visibility"; they remain more readily identifiable for their group characteristics than for their personal attainments.[11] . . .

In order to broaden the study of woman in American history, it is not really necessary to suggest new sources. Primary research material is readily available, not only in the several manuscript collections devoted to the subject, but in the usual primary sources for social historians: local historical records, letters, diaries, the organizational records of women's clubs, religious and charitable organizations, labor unions in fields employing women workers. There are numerous magazines, especially written for women, which provide good source material. Archives of Congress and of state governments contain petitions and statements made at hearings which can yield valuable information about the activities and interests of women. Many of these readily available sources remain neglected.

A fresh approach to known material and to available sources could provide valuable new insights. The following suggestion might make a useful beginning:

First, the subject "Women" is too vast and diffuse to serve as a valid point of departure. Women are members of families, citizens

10 *Society in America* (New York, 1837), I, 158.
11 Helen Hacker, "Women as a Minority Group," *Social Forces,* XXX (1951–1952), 60–69.

of different regions, economic producers, just as men are, but their emphasis on these various roles is different. The economic role of men predominates in their lives, but women shift readily from one role to another at different periods in their lives. It is in this that their function is different from men and it is this which must form the basis for any conceptual framework. In modern society the only statement about women in general which can be made with validity concerns their political status. Therefore the subject should be subsumed under several categories and any inquiry, description, and generalization should be limited to a narrower field. It is useful to deal with the *status* of women at any given time—to distinguish among their economic status, family status, and political-legal status. There must also be a consideration of class position, as has been usefully proven in recent studies of the feminist movement.[12]

Second, we should look at different aspects of women's role in American history. We must certainly be concerned with the woman's-rights movement, but only as part of the total story. Historians must painstakingly restore the actual record of women's contributions at any given period in history. It is interesting that the history of women before the advent of the feminist movement has been more fully recorded and in a more balanced way than it has afterward, so that the story of colonial women can be quite fully traced through secondary literature.[13] But when we deal with the period after 1800, it often proves difficult to establish even descriptive facts. During the early national period, women organized elaborate welfare and relief systems which they staffed and administered. This story should be part of the history of the period; it is not now. Women were the teachers in most of the nation's public schools during the nineteenth century; this is worth recording and exploring. Women made a significant contribution to the growth and development of frontier communities. These are but a few of the many areas in which more research and uncovering of factual information are needed.

Third, we might well discard the "oppressed-group model" when discussing women's role in the political life of the nation. Instead, we might start with the fact that one generalization about women which

---

[12] See Kraditor and Lasch.
[13] A full bibliography of colonial women is to be found in Eugenie A. Leonard, Sophie H. Drinker, and Miriam Y. Holden, *The American Woman in Colonial and Revolutionary Times: 1565–1800* (Philadelphia, 1962).

holds up is that they were, longer than any other group in the nation, deprived of political and economic power. Did this mean they actually wielded no power or did they wield power in different forms? My research has led me to believe that they wielded considerable power and in the middle of the nineteenth century even political power. They found a way to make their power felt through organizations, through pressure tactics, through petitioning, and various other means; these later became models for other mass movements for reform.

Fourth, another important fact is that women are a group who for a considerable period of history were deprived of equal access to education. While they were not illiterate, their education was limited, usually to below the high school level. This was true of the majority of women until the end of the nineteenth century. It might be very useful to investigate what impact this had on female behavior, and more specifically, women's performance as a group in terms of outstanding achievement. To put it another way, how many generations of educated women are necessary to produce a significant number of outstanding women academicians? How many generations of college-trained women are necessary before women in sizable numbers make contributions in the sciences? When do women begin to move from the small-scale, home-centered creative forms, the fiction, poetry, and article-writing, to the larger-scale work within the framework of cultural institutions? Is the proverbial dearth of female philosophers really a result of some innate distinctiveness of female mental function or rather the product of centuries of environmental and institutional deprivation? This type of inquiry lends itself to a comparative cross-cultural approach. A comparison between the educational deprivation of women and that suffered by certain minority groups might lead us to a demonstrable correlation between educational deprivation and a gap of several generations before adequate and competitive performance is possible. This could explain a great deal about some of our problems with minority groups, public schooling, and academic achievement.

Fifth, it would be most worthwhile to distinguish the ideas society held at any given moment in regard to woman's proper "place" from what was actually woman's status at that time. The two do not necessarily overlap. On the contrary, there seems to be a considerable gap between the popular myth and reality. Social historians might legitimately be concerned with the significance of this gap, how to account for it, and whether it fits any distinguishable pattern. It would also be important to understand the function of ideas about women in the general ordering of society. Was the fact that colonial women were idealized as thrifty housewives and able helpmeets cause or effect of the labor shortage in the colonies? Are the idealized suburban housewife, the fashion-conscious teenager, the sex-symbol model, causes or effects of our consumer-oriented society? And what effect does the socially held concept of woman's role have on the development of female talent, on women's contribution to the society?

Finally, we come back to the initial problem of how to judge the contribution of women. Are women noteworthy when their achievement falls exactly in a category of achievement set up for men? Obviously not, for this is how they have been kept out of the history books up to now. Are women noteworthy, then, as the feminists tended to think, if they do anything at all? Not likely. The fact remains that women are different from men and that their role in society and history is different from that of men. Different, but equal in importance. Obviously their achievements must also be measured on a different scale. To define and devise such a scale is difficult until the gaps in our historical knowledge about the actual contributions of women have been filled. This work remains to be done. . . .

II THE COLONIAL AMERICAN EXPERIENCE

Conventional Wisdom

Throughout American history (male) conventional wisdom has been operative in determining the nature of womanhood and female lifestyles.* In the colonial period it was English law, and even more decisively, Puritan/ Protestant religious tenets, which regulated female thought and behavior. The "advice" of the Puritan divine, Cotton Mather, to the women of his day regarding their "character and happiness" is typical. Although colonial women were considered to possess as much (if not more) godliness as men, they were assumed to be lacking in intellect, and made to believe that while they were ultimately created for God, immediately they were designed for men.

Yet for the most part the discrimination against white women was covert. Little is gained by attempting to discover blatant repressive behavior toward women in John Winthrop's or Crèvecoeur's America. With the notable exception of Anne Hutchinson, few other strong-willed women "caused" men to resort to excessive means or outright cruelty. Indeed, the reverse was true. According to the studies of Edmund S. Morgan, fathers were inclined to indulge their daughters; and husbands to give preferential treatment to their wives. As the selections from Crèvecoeur illustrate (with his romanticism aside), the high status of women in colonial America was closely tied to a practical consideration of their vital economic function. (The first third of the essay by Gerda Lerner in Part III explores this subject in some detail.) Of course, the status of black and red women was different. Even a political/ social liberal thinker such as Thomas Jefferson was not immune to the racial attitudes of his day. Although he had some admiration for Indian women and believed they could become "civilized" through intermarriage with white men, like most Americans Jefferson considered black and red women as more akin to animals than human beings. His brief remarks here about blackness apply for the most part to men as well as women.

* Consult Charles Ferguson's neglected work, The Male Attitude (Boston, 1966).

Cotton Mather

ORNAMENTS FOR THE DAUGHTERS OF ZION (1692)

or The Character and Happiness of A Vertuous Woman: In A Discourse Which Directs The Female-Sex how to Express, THE FEAR OF GOD, in every Age and State of their LIFE; and Obtain both Temporal and Eternal Blessedness. . .

Go yee forth now arrayed with such Ornaments as the Apostles have provided for you; Cloath your selves with the Silk of Piety, the Satin of Sanctity, the Purple of Modesty; So the Almighty God will be a Lover of you. . . .

It may well be reckoned the Brightess Honour of that Sex, which the Holy Spirit of God has declar'd Worthy of a Chast and a kind Honour from [Jesus], That when the Fullness of Time was come, God sent forth His Son, made of a Woman. As a Woman had the Disgrace to Go First in that horrid and Woful Transgression of our First Parents, which has been the Parent of all our misery: so a woman had the Glory of bringing into the World this Second Adam, . . .

. . . We may safely account the Female Sex herein more than a little Dignify'd. And how should it Encourage all Women to seek a Saving Interest in That Redeemer, who was Born of a Woman! how should all Women make their Hear[t] a Lodging for that Lord, Who in a Woman received, The Body Prepared for Him! . . .

. . . As one woman was the Mother of Him who is the Essential word of God, so diverse Women have been the writers of His Declarative word. Though the Apostle do's abundantly intimate unto us . . . when he gives the prohibition so much Transgress'd by the most Absurd Sect* in our Dayes, That the Woman may not speak in the Church, Yet our God has Employ'd many Women to write for the Church, and Inspired some of them for the Writing of the Scriptures.

*   *   *

From *Ornaments for the Daughters of Zion, or the Character and Happiness of a Vertuous Woman* (Cambridge, Boston, 1692).

* The Society of Friends.—Ed.

*FAVOUR is Deceitful, and Beauty is Vain;
but a woman that Fears the Lord, Shee
'tis that shall be Praised: [Prov. 31:30]*

The Fear of God is that which is the Heart of a Vertuous Woman is under the Power of. The Female Sex is naturally the Fearful Sex; but the Fear of God is that which Exceeds (and sometimes Extinguishes) all other Fears, . . . It may then be said of a Vertuous Woman, That she is a Religious Woman; she has Bound herself again to that God, Whom she had by the Sin and Fall of her First Mother departed from; She has a Love which do's not cast out the Fear that is no Fault but confirm and seals her in that Fear of God; That all Kind of Piety and Charity is prevailing in her Disposition; That Sobriety and Righteousness and Godliness are visible in her whole Behaviour; and, That she does Justice, loves Mercy, and walks Humbly with her God. . . .

The Fear of God, will Recommend a Woman to the Praise and so to the Choice of such men, as it may be desireable to have the Good Opinion of. For a Woman to be Praised, is for her to be Married, . . .

We say, Matches are made in Heaven; and indeed, the Woman who by the Fear of God, has made sure of a Great interest in Heaven is most like to meet with such a Match as may give her cause to Thank Heaven all her Dayes. Tis possible, That Unsanctify'd men, may Marry only For Portion or for Prettiness; how often do those Respects give us to see Matches made in Hell! and yet there are few men so Profane, as to look upon that Grace as undesireable in a wife, of which they themselves are destitute! But men that have the Fear of God in themselves when they Choose the Companions of their Lives, will ordinarily choose to have such, as they shall hear Praise for. . . .

But shall it now be seen, that Women will more generally aspire after this Character and this Happiness? The petulant Pens of some Froward [sic] and Morose Men, have sometimes treated the Female Sex with very great Indignities; . . . Yet, tis not easy to recount how many Licentious Writers, have handled that Theme, *Femina nulla bona,* No Woman is Good! . . . But, behold, how you may Recover your Impaired Reputation! the Fear of God, will soon make it evident, that you are among, The Excellent in the Earth. If any men are so wicked (and some sects of men have been so) as to deny your being Rational Creatures, the best mean to confuse them, will be by proving yourselves Religious ones. I do assure you, and I have more than Luther to consent and concur with me, in this Assertion, That the Actions of even the meanest Milkmaid or Cook maid, when done in the Fear of God, are in the Account of God more Noble Things than the Victories of a Caesar! . . .

. . . Tis plain, that as there were three Maries to one John, standing under the Cross of our Dying Lord, so still there are far more Godly women in the World then there are Godly Men; and our Church Communions give us a Little Demonstration of it. I have seen it without going a Mile from home; That in a Church of between Three or Four Hundred Communicants, there are but few more than One Hundred Men, all the Rest are Women. . . . It seems that the Curse in the Difficulties both of Subjection and of Child bearing, which the Female Sex is doom'd unto, has been turn'd into a Blessing, by the Free Grace of our most Gracious God. God sanctifies the Chains, the Pains, the Deaths which they meet withal; and furthermore, makes the Tenderness of their Disposition, a Further Occasion of Serious Devotion in them. . . . And Let me tell you, That most of You, have more Time to Employ in the more Immediate Service of your Souls, than the Other Sex is owner of. You are Ordinarily more within the House, and so may more mind the Work within the Heart, than we. . . .

While you thus maintain the, Fear of God, Let it very particularly discover itself in your Keeping the purpose of the Psalmist, *I will take heed unto my ways that I Sin not with my Tongue; I will Keep my Mouth with a Bridle.* May it be as much, a causeless, as it is a Common, Report concerning you, that your Tongues are frequently not so Governed by the, Fear of God, as they ought to be. The Faculty of Speech is of such a Noble and of such a signal Figure in the Constitution of Mankind, that it is a thousand pitties, it should be Abus'd, but Woman Kind is usually charged with a peculiar share in the Worlds Abuses of it. It is indeed a piece of great Injustice, that every Woman should be so far an Eve, as that her Depravation should be imputed unto all the Sex. Nevertheless it highly concerns you to do your part that . . . you may be better spoken of, as to the matter of your speaking. . . . Be careful that you don't Speak too soon, because you cannot fetch back and eat up, what is uttered; but Study to Answer. And be careful that you don't Speak too much, because that when the Chest is always open, everyone counts there are no Treasure in it; and the Scripture tells us, 'tis the Whore, that is Clamorous, and the Fool, that is Full of Words.

* * *

. . . She betimes applies herself to Learn all the Affairs of House-wifry and besides a good skill at her Needle, as well as in the Kitchen, she acquaints her self with Arithmetick and Accomptantship (perhaps also Chirurgery*) and such other Arts relating to Business, as may Enable her to do the Man whom she may hereafter have, Good and not Evil, all the Days of her Life. If she have any Time after this to Learn Musick and Language she will not Loose her Time, and yet she will not be proud of her Skill, though the Name of Lora, that is Learning, . . . should justly belong unto her. She would with all good Accomplishments be a Ruth, which is to say, A Filled One. . . .

. . . Her Fidelity is no where more signalized, than in her sollici-tude for the Eternal Salvation of her Husband; O how Unwilling she is that the Precious and Immortal Soul of her Poor Husband, should go from her Arms, to make his Bed among the Dragons of the Wilderness For ever! . . . Truly, though a Woman may not speak in the Church, yet she may humbly Repeat unto her husband at Home what the Minister spoke in the Church that may be Pertinent unto his Condition. . . . If her Husband be a Carnal, Prayerless, Graceless man, she will not leave off her Ingenious Perswasions, till it may be said of him, Behold, he Prayes! . . . She pursues him with Loving, Winning, Unwearied Sollicitations, to, Fear God, and, Serve God, and, Never be weary of well doing. Instead of being a Delilah, that shall Entangle him in the Cords of Death, she do's all she can to be a Priscilla, that shall more fully acquaint him, with the Things per-taining to the Kingdom of God.

This, is a Vertuous wife! And Such an One She will be although her Husband should be very Disobliging to her; she considers, Tis to the Lord. I Confess the Difficulties that some Unhappy wives do meet withal, are such, that if they be not very Vertuous Wives, they cannot possibly Conform to these Directions; but this I would say, their being Vertuous is the most Likely way to provide against their being Unhappy.

* Surgery.—Ed.

Hector St. John De Crèvecoeur
ON EIGHTEENTH-CENTURY WOMANHOOD (1782)

. . . I married, and this perfectly reconciled me to my situation; my wife rendered my house all at once cheerful and pleasing; it no longer appeared gloomy and solitary as before; when I went to work in my fields, I worked with more alacrity and sprightliness; I felt that I did not work for myself alone, and this encouraged me much. My wife would often come with her knitting in her hand and sit under the shady tree, praising the straightness of my furrows and the docility of my horses; this swelled my heart and made everything light and pleasant, and I regretted that I had not married before. . . .

When I contemplate my wife, by my fire-side, while she either spins, knits, darns, or suckles our child, I cannot describe the various emotions of love, of gratitude, of conscious pride, which thrill in my heart and often overflow in involuntary tears. I feel the necessity, the sweet pleasure of acting my part, the part of an husband and father, with an attention and propriety which may entitle me to my good fortune. It is true these pleasing images vanish with the smoke of my pipe, but though they disappear from my mind, the impression they have made on my heart is indelible. . . .

. . . As I observed before, every man takes a wife as soon as he chooses, and that is generally very early; no portion is required, none is expected; no marriage articles are drawn up among us by skilful lawyers to puzzle and lead posterity to the bar or to satisfy the pride of the parties. We give nothing with our daughters; their education, their health, and the customary outset are all that the fathers of numerous families can afford. As the wife's fortune consists principally in her future economy, modesty, and skilful management, so the husband's is founded on his abilities to labor, on his health, and the knowledge of some trade or business. Their mutual endeavors, after a few years of constant application, seldom fail of success and of bringing them the means to rear and support the new race which accompanies the nuptial bed. . . .

From *Letters from an American Farmer* (New York, 1912); *Sketches of Eighteenth Century America,* edited by H. L. Bourdin, R. H. Gabriel, and S. T. Williams (New Haven, 1925).

FIGURE 1. The relatively high status of white women in colonial America was closely tied to a practical appreciation of their vital economic role. *(Historical Pictures Service, Chicago)*

The tenants of his house, like the beasts of his farm, must now depend on the collected stores of the preceding season, sagaciously distributed and prepared by the industry of his wife. There lies the "aurum potabile" of an American farmer. He may work and gather the choicest fruits of his farm; but if female economy fails, he loses the comfort of good victuals. He sees wholesome meats, excellent flours converted into indifferent food; whilst his neighbor, more happy, though less rich, feeds on well-cooked dishes, well-composed puddings. For such is our lot: if we are blessed with a good wife, we may boast of living better than any people of the same rank on the globe. . . .

It is in the art of our simple cookery that our wives all aim at distinguishing themselves. This wife is famous for one thing, that for the other. She who has not fresh comb-honey, some sweetmeats of her own composing, and smoked beef at tea would be looked upon as very inexpert indeed. Thus these light repasts become on every account the most expensive of any; and as we dine early and work until tea-time, they often are very serious meals at which abundance of biscuits and shortcakes are always eaten. . . .

In the future details which I intend to give you of our modes of living, of our different home manufactures, of the different resources which an industrious family must find within itself, you'll be better able to judge what a useful acquisition a good wife is to an American farmer, and how small is his chance of prosperity if he draws a blank in that lottery! . . .

Thomas Jefferson
ON INDIAN AND BLACK WOMEN (1781–82)

. . . The [Indian] women are submitted to unjust drudgery. This I believe is the case with every barbarous people. With such, force is law. The stronger sex therefore imposes on the weaker. It is civilization alone which replaces women in the enjoyment of their natural equality. That first teaches us to subdue the selfish passions, and to respect those rights in others which we value in ourselves. Were we in equal barbarism, our females would be equal drudges. The man with them is less strong than with us, but their women stronger than ours; and both for the same obvious reason; because our man and their woman is habituated to labor, and formed by it. With both races the sex which is indulged with ease is least athletic. An Indian man is small in the hand and wrist, for the same reason for which a sailor is large and strong in the arms and shoulders, and a porter in

From *Notes on the State of Virginia* (Boston, 1832).

the legs and thighs. They raise fewer children than we do. The causes of this are to be found, not in a difference of nature, but of circumstance. The women very frequently attending the men in their parties of war and of hunting, child-bearing becomes extremely inconvenient to them. It is said, therefore, that they have learned the practice of procuring abortion by the use of some vegetable; and that it even extends to prevent conception for a considerable time after. During these parties they are exposed to numerous hazards, to excessive exertions, and to the greatest extremities of hunger. Even at their homes the nation depends for food, through a certain part of every year, on the gleanings of the forest: that is, they experience a famine once in every year. With all animals, if the female be badly fed, or not fed at all, her young perish; and if both male and female be reduced to like want, generation becomes less active, less productive. To the obstacles then of want and hazard, which nature has opposed to the multiplication of wild animals, for the purpose of restraining their numbers within certain bounds, those of labor and of voluntary abortion are added with the Indian. No wonder then if they multiply less than we do. Where food is regularly supplied, a single farm will show more of cattle, than a whole country of forests can of buffaloes. The same Indian women, when married to white traders, who feed them and their children plentifully and regularly, who exempt them from excessive drudgery, who keep them stationary and unexposed to accident, produce and raise as many children as the white women.

*   *   *

. . . The first difference which strikes us is that of color.—Whether the black of the negro resides in the reticular membrane between the skin and scarf-skin, or in the scarf-skin itself; whether it proceeds from the color of the blood, the color of the bile, or from that of some other secretion, the difference is fixed in nature, and is as real as if its seat and cause were better known to us. And is this difference of no importance? Is it not the foundation of a greater or less share of beauty in the two races? Are not the fine mixtures of red and white, the expressions of every passion by greater or less suffusions of color in the one, preferable to that eternal monotony, which reigns in the countenances, that immovable veil of black which covers all the emotions of the other race? Add to these, flowing hair, a more elegant symmetry of form, their own judgment in favor of the whites, declared by their preference of them, as uniformly as is the preference of the Oranootan for the black women over those of his own species. The circumstance of superior beauty, is thought worthy attention in the propagation of our horses, dogs, and other domestic animals; why not in that of man? Besides those of color, figure, and hair, there are other physical distinctions proving a difference of race. They have less hair on the face and body. They secrete less by the kidneys, and more by the glands of the skin, which gives them a very strong and disagreeable odor. . . .

. . . In general, their existence appears to participate more of sensation than reflection. To this must be ascribed their disposition to sleep when abstracted from their diversions, and unemployed in labor. An animal whose body is at rest, and who does not reflect, must be disposed to sleep of course. Comparing them by their faculties of memory, reason, and imagination, it appears to me, that in memory they are equal to the whites; in reason much inferior, as I think one could scarcely be found capable of tracing and comprehending the investigations of Euclid; and that in imagination they are dull, tasteless, and anomalous. . . . Never yet could I find that a black had uttered a thought above the level of plain narration; never see even an elementary trait of painting or sculpture. In music they are more generally gifted than the whites with accurate ears for tune and time, and they have been found capable of imagining a small catch. Whether they will be equal to the composition of a more extensive run of melody, or of complicated harmony, is yet to be proved. Misery is often the parent of the most affecting touches in poetry.—Among the blacks is misery enough, God knows, but no poetry. Love is the peculiar oestrum of the poet. Their love is ardent, but it kindles the senses only, not the imagination. Religion indeed has produced a Phyllis Whately [1753–1784]; but it could not produce a poet. The compositions published under her name are below the dignity of criticism.

Critical Appraisal

Ann Stanford
ANNE BRADSTREET: DOGMATIST AND REBEL

The following essay about poet Anne Bradstreet provides us with an oppor-tunity to obtain a glimpse of the unarticulated responses which many colo-nial women must have had toward the daily, subtle discrimination which they experienced in common. While keeping their innermost thoughts care-fully guarded, many women must have questioned their prescribed status and the equation of womanhood with intellectual inferiority. Specifically, Professor Ann Stanford's study of one woman is a model for coming to terms with the tensions that many Puritan women encountered in attempt-ing to reconcile male standards of authority with their own private feelings as persons. On the one hand, they were expected as dutiful Christians to affirm right belief over self-interest, the head over the heart, and the spiritual over the aspirations of the flesh. Yet, like Anne Bradstreet, they probably were ambivalent in their loyalties and struggled with concurrent feelings of submission and resistance. In contrast to the outspoken Anne Hutchinson, the quiet rebellion of Anne Bradstreet as a self-proclaimed writer and poet was different only in degree, not in kind, from that of other women. Ann Stanford (b. 1942) is both a poet and teacher, a graduate of the University of California at Los Angeles, specializing in American literature.

When in the summer of 1630 Anne Bradstreet looked from the deck of the *Arbella* at the crude settlement of Salem, Massachusetts, it was no doubt a dismal sight compared to her own homeland—the flat, fen country of Lincolnshire, with its towns and great estates. She later told how she "came into this Country, where I found a new world and new manners, at which my heart rose," that is, her heart rebelled. "But after I was convinced it was the way of God, I sub-mitted to it and joined to the church at Boston."

The elements of this first reaction were to be repeated again and again during Anne Bradstreet's pilgrimage through the new world. There was the rising of the heart either in dismay or rebellion and

Reprinted by permission from *The New England Quarterly* (September, 1966), pp. 373–389. Footnotes omitted.

the assertion of the self against the dogma she encountered. Next, there was the need for conviction. It was only after persuasion that she could ever submit to the "way." Rebellion and a struggle for or against conviction form a pattern which runs through her writing. It is the statement of dogma and the concurrent feeling of resistance to dogma that give much of that writing the vitality we are still conscious of today.

The very fact that she wrote, that she considered herself a poet, that she continued to write in spite of criticism, indicates that she was willing to act independently in spite of the dogmatic assertions of many of her contemporaries, even those of the venerable John Winthrop. Winthrop recorded in his journal for April 13, 1645, the following comment on Anne Hopkins:

> *Mr. Hopkins, the governour of Hartford upon Connecticut, came to Boston, and brought his wife with him (a godly young woman, and of special parts), who was fallen into a sad infirmity, the loss of her understanding and reason, which had been growing upon her divers years, by occasion of her giving herself wholly to reading and writing, and had written many books. Her husband, being very loving and tender of her, was loath to grieve her; but he saw his errour, when it was too late. For if she had attended her household affairs, and such things as belong to women, and not gone out of her way and calling to meddle in such things as are proper for men, whose minds are stronger &c. she had kept her wits, and might have improved them usefully and honourably in the place God had set her.*

And Thomas Parker wrote to his sister in a public letter, published in London, 1650, "your printing of a Book, beyond the custom of your Sex, doth rankly smell."

Anne Bradstreet had already encountered such attitudes when, in 1642, she wrote in her "Prologue" to "The Four Elements":

> *I am obnoxious to each carping tongue*
> *Who says my hand a needle better fits,*
> *A Poets pen all scorn I should thus wrong,*
> *For such despite they cast on Female wits:*
> *If what I do prove well, it won't advance,*
> *They'l say it's stoln, or else it was by chance.*

She goes on to point out that to the Greeks the Nine Muses were women and Poesy itself was *"Calliope's* own Child." But, she says, to this argument her critics reply that "the Greeks did nought, but play the fools & lye." She then makes her customary concession to current dogma:

> Let Greeks be Greeks, and women what they are
> Men have precedency and still excell,
> It is but vain unjustly to wage warre;
> Men can do best, and women know it well
> Preheminence in all and each is yours.

The preeminence of man over woman was for both Anglican and Puritan a God-given condition. St. Paul had asserted it, and the authority of the man, especially in the state of marriage, was the subject of much discussion among Protestant ministers. This subject was of particular theological interest because of the development of the Protestant idea of a married clergy. Anne Bradstreet had doubtless heard sermons to this effect, and perhaps had read books on domestic relations such as those of Thomas Gataker: *A Good Wife, God's Gift* (1620), and *Marriage Duties Briefly Couched Together* (1620). She was as well aware as Milton that men and women were

> Not equal, as thir sex not equal seemd;
> For contemplation hee and valour formd,
> For softness shee and sweet attractive Grace,
> Hee for God only, shee for God in him.
> (P. L., *iv, 296–299*)

And she, like Eve, knew

> How beauty is excelled by manly grace
> And wisdom.
> (P. L., *iv, 490–491*)

Yet for Anne Bradstreet this dogma did not mean that women were not to use their wits at all. After admitting that men are superior, she asks them to "grant some small acknowledgement of ours." In other words, she would not have women confined to household affairs to the extent expected by John Winthrop.

In the following year, in her elegy on Queen Elizabeth, she stated her belief in the intellectual capacity of women much more strongly:

> *Nay Masculines, you have thus taxt us long,*
> *But she, though dead, will vindicate our wrong.*
> *Let such as say our Sex is void of Reason,*
> *Know tis a Slander now, but once was Treason.*

And despite the carping tongues, she kept on writing. . . .

However, Anne Bradstreet was careful not to make the mistake of Anne Hopkins. She did not neglect her domestic affairs. The author of the preface to her book, *The Tenth Muse,* assures the "Kind Reader" that this is the "Work of a Woman, honoured, and esteemed where she lives, for her gracious demeanour, her eminent parts, her pious conversation, her courteous disposition, her exact diligence in her place, and discreet managing of her Family occasions." Furthermore, the author assures the reader that these poems were not written during hours which should have been devoted to work, but "are the fruit but of some few houres, curtailed from her sleep and other refreshments."

Thus, because she did observe in her conduct an exact conformity to the mores of her community, Anne Bradstreet was able to continue to write though the practice of writing by women was disapproved of by many in the community and by the governor himself.

Her first book *The Tenth Muse* was published in London in 1650, the year that Thomas Parker criticized his sister for the "printing of a Book." Anne Bradstreet was protected from such criticism by the fact that the book was brought out without her knowledge, as her editor is careful to assert. Her reaction to the publication, however, was not so much annoyance at having her poems "expos'd to publick view" as it was that they were brought to public view "in raggs, halting to th' press." Her concern was with the blemishes in her work, and with the fact that the printer increased the errors. She set out to correct these flaws; the second edition, published six years after her death, states on the title page that it is "Corrected by the Author."

Thus in her determination to write and in her defense of the capability of women to reason, to contemplate, and to read widely, she showed herself capable of taking a stand against the more conservative and dogmatic of her contemporaries. It was a quiet rebellion, carried on as an undercurrent in an atmosphere of conformity.

Further examples of this tendency toward independence carried on under the guise and beneath repeated statements of dogma occur in the case of the three early elegies and the poems she wrote to her husband. The elegies are written in the form of funeral poems for Sir Philip Sidney, Queen Elizabeth and the French poet, Du Bartas. They are modeled on similar elegies found in Joshua Sylvester's work. But Sylvester concludes his elegies with a Christian apotheosis: the reader should not mourn, since the dead is with the saints in heaven. There is little of heaven in Anne Bradstreet's elegies. The apotheosis for the three characters she celebrates is not a higher Christian transformation, but fame. In such promise, she is closer to the classic poets and the Cavaliers than to the other Puritan writers. . . .

These poems promise a continuation of the individual life on this earth through fame. The same attitude runs through the poems to her husband and children, though the earthly fame is to be continued in a different manner. One of the interesting poems with regard to this point is that titled "Before the Birth of one of her Children." The poem suggests she may die, and the reader assumes she is thinking of the possibility of death in childbirth. She asks her husband to forget her faults and remember what virtues she may have had. Here, as in so many of her poems, there is a conflict between her acceptance of Puritan dogma, and her own warm personality. She states her awareness that life is brief and joys are apt to be followed by adversity. But she also says

> *love bids me*
> *These farewell lines to recommend to thee,*
> *That when that knot's unty'd that made us one,*
> *I may seem thine, who in effect am none.*

It was the Puritan belief that a marriage was dissolved at death. Marriage was for the earthly life only, and in afterlife any union between spirits was no longer in effect. A person must not love any earthly thing too much, and even excessive grief for a departed spouse or child was contrary to God's command, since it showed that one had too much regard for the things of this world. Anne Bradstreet voiced the Puritan view when she spoke of untying the knot "that made us one," just as she expressed it in the last line of another poem to her husband when she said, "Let's still remain but one till death divide." But she tries to get around the idea of the complete severance of death by writing lines so that "I may seem

thine, who in effect am none." Despite the Puritan idea of the end
of love in death, she wants to be remembered on this earth; she
admits that her husband will probably marry again, as was customary, but she still hopes that

> *if chance to thine eyes shall bring this verse,*
> *With some sad sighs honour my absent Herse;*
> *And kiss this paper for thy loves dear sake. . . .*

. . . The desires for fame, honor, and worldly remembrance, indeed,
seem to be special temptations for Anne Bradstreet. In her dialogue
between "The Flesh and the Spirit" these are included among the
temptations that Flesh sets forth:

> *Dost honour like? acquire the same,*
> *As some to their immortal fame:*
> *And trophyes to thy name erect*
> *Which wearing time shall ne're deject.*

The Spirit properly and dogmatically rejects such temptations:

> *Thy sinfull pleasures I doe hate,*
> *Thy riches are to me no bait,*
> *Thine honours doe, nor will I love;*
> *For my ambition lyes above.*
> *My greatest honour it shall be.*
> *When I am victor over thee.*

The Spirit here has taken the proper Puritan attitude toward
earthly things, but the Flesh clings to the visible. The struggle is
recorded by Anne Bradstreet in prose as well as in poetry. God and
his world to come are invisible, and Anne Bradstreet is reluctant to
place her trust in either the actuality of God or the reality of life
after death. She wrote in her notebook: "Many times hath Satan
troubled me concerning the verity of the scriptures, many times by
Atheisme how I could know whether there was a God; I never saw
any miracles to confirm me, and those which I read of how did I know
but they were feigned." These questions are not unique in Anne
Bradstreet; other good Puritans such as Thomas Shepard and John
Bunyan also asked them. But the elaborateness with which Anne
Bradstreet formulates her answers indicates that for her too they

were genuine problems. It is true that in the complete passage she does resolve her doubts through a determination to rely upon faith: "Return, O my Soul, to thy Rest, upon this Rock Christ Jesus will I build my faith." But she adds, "and, if I perish, I perish." So it takes one more assertion to close the argument: "But I know all the Powers of Hell shall never prevail against it. I know whom I have trusted . . . and that he is able to keep that I have committed to his charge." . . .

The struggle between dogma and feeling reaches its apex in the seven poems composed between 1665 and 1670, the last years of Anne Bradstreet's life. These include two personal poems and four memorial elegies upon members of her family.

These last poems present the arguments of the Flesh and the Spirit in relation to real occurrences. The Flesh argued for the visible against the invisible, and for honor, wealth, and pleasure. But what the real woman wants, rather than riches, is a home with its comforts and memories; rather than honor and pleasure, the lives of loved ones; and finally life itself. In these poems, Anne Bradstreet presents her own conflict in regard to these desires. Her feelings about her home represent the most material conflict. In 1666, when the Bradstreet home at Andover burned down, she wrote a poem about the conflagration and her own feelings. She describes her awakening to the "shreiks of dreadfull voice" and going out to watch "the flame consume" her "dwelling place." But she comforts herself with good Puritan dogma:

> *And, when I could no longer look,*
> *I blest his Name that gave and took,*
> *That layd my goods now in the dust:*
> *Yea so it was, and so 'twas just.*
> *It was his own: it was not mine;*
> *Far be it that I should repine.*
>
> *He might of All justly bereft,*
> *But yet sufficient for us left.*

This is an argument that Spirit might have used; the burning of the house was God's doing, and his doings should not be questioned. But she *does* question in the next three stanzas, where she lovingly goes over the contents of the house—the questioning being

through feeling tone rather than statement. As she passes the ruins,
she recreates the pleasant things that had been there:

> *When by the Ruines oft I past,*
> *My sorrowing eyes aside did cast,*
> *And here and there the places spye*
> *Where oft I sate, and long did lye.*
>
> *Here stood that Trunk, and there that chest;*
> *There lay that store I counted best:*
> *My pleasant things in ashes lye,*
> *And them behold no more shall I.*
> *Under thy roof no guest shall sitt,*
> *Nor at thy Table eat a bitt.*
>
> *No pleasant tale shall 'ere be told,*
> *Nor things recounted done of old.*
> *No candle 'ere shall shine in Thee,*
> *Nor bridegroom's voice ere heard shall bee.*

In its progress the poem becomes almost another dialogue of dogma
and feeling, or of Flesh and Spirit, for she chides her own heart in
the manner of the Spirit:

> *Then streight I 'gin my heart to chide,*
> *And did thy wealth on earth abide?*
> *Didst fix thy hope on mouldring dust,*
> *The arm of flesh didst make thy trust?*
> *Raise up thy thoughts above the skye*
> *That dunghill mists away may flie.*
>
> *Thou hast an house on high erect,*
> *Fram'd by that mighty Architect,*
> *With glory richly furnished,*
> *Stands permanent tho: this bee fled.*

Despite the reasonable arguments that her goods belonged to God
and whatever God does is just, there is in the poem an undercurrent
of regret that the loss is not fully compensated for by the hope of
treasure that lies above.

The undercurrent is even stronger in the elegies on her grand-
children. Though dogma could reason that God could take away her
possessions, and though she could accept this on a rational level,

even though it ran counter to her feelings, what could Spirit say when God took away her dearest relatives? The questioning extends over the last four elegies. . . .

. . . There is in these a strong note of personal bereavement, which goes beyond the impersonal tone of earlier poems, and that of the period generally: there is an inclination to use "self-expression," in itself a move in the direction of later writers, in interpreting these deaths in their relation to herself. The first elegy is on Elizabeth who died at the age of one and a half. It is incidentally one of the finest elegies in American literature. Here she admits in keeping with dogma that her heart was set too much on one who was after all only one of God's creatures:

> Farewel dear babe, my hearts too much content,
> Farewel sweet babe, the pleasure of mine eye,
> Farewel fair flower that for a space was lent,
> Then ta'en away unto Eternity.

She concludes the stanza with a conventional question:

> Blest babe why should I once bewail thy fate,
> Or sigh the dayes so soon were terminate;
> Sith thou art setled in an Everlasting state.

This should lead into a conventional Christian apotheosis, but the problem for Anne Bradstreet is that she cannot properly, i.e. dogmatically, answer the question. She answers it by stating how she really feels instead of how she *should* feel. . . . So she concludes, not by joy in the Christian transformation, but by a backing down from her near-criticism of the deity, and says that the taking away of this fair flower "is by his hand alone that guides nature and fate." . . .

Of more interest in showing the final real outcome of the dialogue of Flesh and Spirit is the poem written in the summer of 1669, usually called "A Pilgrim." It was composed in the same summer as the conventional and world-weary poem on the death of her second grandchild. In it she considers the loss of the flesh itself, that is her own earthly life. Here the Flesh has already lost out; there is no internal conflict; only the inconveniences of the Flesh are considered:

>   This body shall in silence sleep
>   Mine eyes no more shall ever weep
>   No fainting fits shall me assaile
>   nor grinding paines my body fraile
>   With cares and fears ne'r cumbred be
>   Nor losses know, nor sorrowes see.

*   *   *

In the final analysis the spirit wins because it can outlast the flesh, and the individual submits to the loss of the flesh and the hope of the resurrection because he must. As when she first came into the country, Anne Bradstreet was always willing to submit to the inevitable during her long pilgrimage, but she did it only after using the full faculties of the soul—the imagination, the affections, and the will—and it is this clash of feeling and dogma that keeps her poetry alive. True, her tension is often resolved, and it is without the darkness, alienation, and disorder that grows out of the tension in later American writers. But Anne Bradstreet went as far as her place in a society which condemned Anne Hutchinson and Anne Hopkins would allow. . . .

Further Reading

Professor Stanford has used *The Works of Anne Bradstreet in Prose and Verse* edited by John Harvard Ellis (Charlestown, Mass., 1867) as a basis for her discussion of Anne Bradstreet. In part, Stanford's broader conceptual framework is indebted to the studies of Richard Chase, *The American Novel and Its Tradition* (New York, 1957), and D. H. Lawrence, *Studies in Classic American Literature* (Garden City, N.Y., 1951). For an understanding of the dynamic of Puritan society see Edmund S. Morgan's *The Puritan Family: Religious and Domestic Relations in Seventeenth-Century New England* (New York, 1946), and his *The Puritan Dilemma: The Story of John Winthrop* (Boston, 1958), which also deals with the significance of Anne Hutchinson for the Puritan experiment. The general subject of family life in colonial New England has received some attention from historians. Consult James A. Henretta's "The Morphology of New England Society in the Colonial Period," *Journal of Interdisciplinary History* (Autumn, 1971), which reviews family studies by John Demos, Philip J. Greven, Jr., Kenneth A. Lockridge and Michael Zuckerman. To understand another side of the outcome of the struggle between "the flesh and spirit" see Kai Erikson, *Wayward Puritans: A Study in the Sociology of Deviance* (New York, 1966), and Emil Oberholzer, *Delinquent Saints: Disciplinary Action in the Early Congregational Churches of Massachusetts* (New York, 1956).

Winthrop D. Jordan

FRUITS OF PASSION:
THE DYNAMICS OF INTERRACIAL SEX

Winthrop D. Jordan (b. 1931), professor of history at the University of California at Berkeley, has written the definitive study of the genesis of racial attitudes in America before 1812. In his book White Over Black *Jordan suggests that white self-consciousness was already present at an initial stage in the attitudinal development of transplanted Englishmen. Rooted in earlier European contacts with Africans and reinforced by biblical mythology, white racial patterns in the colonies associated the black person's color with disease and the notions of inferiority and evil. Yet at the same time, as Professor Jordan points out in the following selection, the English colonists were caught up in an irreconcilable conflict between their desire for, and their aversion to, interracial sexual union. Although no one believed that intermixture was a good thing, miscegenation was practiced extensively in all the English colonies. The contradiction between utterance and reality regarding miscegenation was not limited to marginal male behavior but embraced men of high ideals such as Thomas Jefferson. Indeed, the tensions and confusion generated by the dynamic of interracial sex not only affected its victims—in a sense, white women and black men as well as black women—but had tragic consequences for all of American society as well. Increasingly throughout the colonial period the guilt and fear of reprisal produced by widespread white aggressive male sexuality toward black women assisted in shaping masculine modes of thought and behavior which eventually created a system of exploitation unequaled in the history of slavery in the Western world.*

When Europeans met Africans in America the result was slavery, revolt, the sociability of daily life, and, inevitably, sexual union. The blending of black and white began almost with the first contact of the two peoples and has far outlasted the institution of chattel slavery. It became, in some English colonies, almost an institution in itself. It rivaled the slave revolt as a source of tension. It may even have equaled the pressure of daily contact as a mechanism of cultural fusion. Most important, however, was the reticular complex of tensions which arose concerning interracial mixture. . . .

Miscegenation was extensive in all the English colonies, a fact

Reprinted from the first part of Chapter 4 of *White Over Black: American Attitudes Toward the Negro, 1550–1812* (Chapel Hill, 1968), with the permission of the University of North Carolina Press and the Institute of Early American History and Culture. Footnotes omitted.

made evident to contemporaries by the presence of large numbers of mulattoes. It is impossible to ascertain how much intermixture there actually was, though it seems likely there was more during the eighteenth century than at any time since. Although miscegenation was probably most common among the lower orders, white men of every social rank slept with Negro women. The colonists, as well as European travelers in the colonies, frequently pointed to this facet of American life.

No one thought intermixture was a good thing. Rather, English colonials were caught in the push and pull of an irreconcilable conflict between desire and aversion for interracial sexual union. The perceptual prerequisite for this conflict is so obvious as to be too easily overlooked: desire and aversion rested on the bedrock fact that white men perceived Negroes as being *both alike and different* from themselves. Without perception of similarity, no desire and no widespread gratification was possible. Without perception of difference, on the other hand, no aversion to miscegenation nor tension concerning it could have arisen. Without perception of difference, of course, the term *miscegenation* had no meaning. Given the simultaneous feelings of desire and aversion, it seems probable that of the two the latter is more demanding of explanation. The sexual drive of human beings has always, in the long run, overridden even the strongest sense of difference between two groups of human beings and, in some individuals, has even overriden the far stronger sense which men have of the difference between themselves and animals. What demands explanation, in short, is why there was any aversion among the white colonists to sexual union with Negroes. More than desire, aversion was a manifestation of cultural rather than biological patterns, so that the answers may be looked for in the qualities of the various cultural settings which were emerging in English America and to the prevailing patterns of miscegenation which constituted important elements in New World cultural styles.

In most colonies virtually all the offspring of these unions were illegitimate, but legally sanctified interracial marriages did occur, especially though not exclusively in New England. Miscegenation in colonial America, as has been true since, typically involved fornication between white men and Negro women, though the inverse combination was common, far more common than is generally supposed. Probably a majority of interracial marriages in New

England involved Negro men and white women of "the meaner sort."
In the plantation colonies, though there were occasional instances
of white women marrying Negroes, legitimization of this relationship
was unusual. Yet white men were sometimes left to ponder indignities such as that suffered (and in return imposed) by a Maryland
man who advertised in 1759 that he would no longer be responsible
for his wife's debts because *"Mary Skinner,* my Wife, has, after all
the Love and Tenderness which could possibly be shown by Man to
a Woman, polluted my Bed, by taking to her in my Stead, her own
Negro Slave, by whom she hath a Child, which hath occasioned so
much Disgrace to me and my Family, that I have thought proper to
forbid her my Sight any more."

Public feeling about miscegenation was strong enough to force
itself over the hurdles of the legislative process into the statute
books of many English continental colonies. As early as the 1660s
the Maryland and Virginia assemblies had begun to lash out at miscegenation in language dripping with distaste and indignation. By
the turn of the century it was clear in many continental colonies that
the English settlers felt genuine revulsion for interracial sexual union,
at least in principle. About 1700 the Chester County Court in Pennsylvania ordered a Negro "never more to meddle with any white woman
more uppon paine of his life." Statutory prohibitions roughly similar
to those of the tobacco colonies and Bermuda were adopted by
Massachusetts in 1705, North Carolina in 1715, South Carolina in
1717, Pennsylvania in 1726, and by Georgia when Negroes were
admitted to the colony in 1750. Delaware enacted no outright prohibition but prescribed heavier fines for interracial bastardy cases
than for such cases involving two white persons. Thus two northern
and all the plantation colonies legally prohibited miscegenation. Community feeling was of course not monolithically arrayed against interracial union: in 1699 several citizens petitioned the Virginia Council for repeal of the intermarriage prohibition, and as late as 1755
the North Carolina Assembly responded favorably to a petition by
inhabitants from several counties asking repeal of the laws in which
"free Negroes and Mulatto's Intermarrying with white women are
obliged to pay taxes for their wives and families." In general, though,
the weight of community opinion was set heavily against the sexual
union of white and black, as the long-standing statutory prohibitions
indicated. Even in South Carolina, where interracial liaisons were

less carefully concealed than elsewhere on the continent, a grand jury in 1743 publicly condemned "THE TOO COMMON PRAC- TICE of CRIMINAL CONVERSATION with NEGRO and other SLAVE WENCHES IN THIS PROVINCE, as an Enormity and Evil of general Ill-Consequence." In significant contrast, none of the West Indian assemblies prohibited extramarital miscegenation and only one took the probably unnecessary step of banning racial intermarriage.

In the West Indian colonies especially, and less markedly in South Carolina, the entire pattern of miscegenation was far more inflexible than in the other English settlements. White women in the islands did not sleep with Negro men, let alone marry them. Nor did white men actually marry Negroes or mulattoes: as one usually temperate planter declared, "The very idea is shocking." Yet white men com- monly, almost customarily, took Negro women to bed with little pre- tense at concealing the fact. Colored mistresses were kept openly. "The Planters are in general rich," a young traveler wrote, "but a set of dissipating, abandoned, and cruel people. Few even of the married ones, but keep a Mulatto or Black Girl in the house or at lodgings for certain purposes." Edward Long of Jamaica described the situ- ation more vividly: "He who should presume to shew any displeasure against such a thing as simple fornication, would for his pains be accounted a simple blockhead; since not one in twenty can be per- suaded, that there is either sin; or shame in cohabiting with his slave." Negro concubinage was an integral part of island life, tightly interwoven into the social fabric.

It is scarcely necessary to resort to speculation about the influence of tropical climate in order to explain this situation, for life in the islands was in large degree shaped by the enormous disproportion of Negroes to white settlers and characterized by the concomitant brutal nakedness of planter domination over the slaves. In the West Indian islands and to less extent South Carolina, racial slavery consisted of unsheathed dominion by relatively small numbers of white men over enormous numbers of Negroes, and it was in these colonies that Negro men were most stringently barred from sexual relations with white women. Sexually as well as in every other way, Negroes were utterly subordinated. White men extended their dominion over their Negroes to the bed, where the sex act itself served as ritualistic reenactment of the daily pattern of social dominance. In New En- gland, at the other extreme, white men had no need for aggressive assertion of their dominance in order to sustain slavery on a major scale and hence in New England Negro men were accorded some measure of sexual freedom. . . .

. . . Miscegenation probably did not seem so much a matter of long-term discoloration as an immediate failure to live up to im-memorial standards. Here again, the intentions which drove English overseas expansion were of crucial importance. The colonists' con-viction that they must sustain their civilized condition wherever they went rendered miscegenation *ipso facto* a negation of the under-lying plan of settlement in America. Simply because most Negroes were chattel slaves, racial amalgamation was stamped as irredeem-ably illicit; it was irretrievably associated with loss of control over the baser passions, with weakening of traditional family ties, and with breakdown of proper social ordering. Judge Sewall's "orderly Families" were rendered a mockery by fathers taking slave wenches to bed.

At the same time it would be absurd to suppose that the status of Negroes in itself aroused American aversion to intermixture and that the physical difference in Negroes was of slight importance. Without that difference there could never have developed well-formulated conceptions about sexual relations between Africans and Europeans in America. Although perhaps there was some feeling that the laws which prevented racial intermingling helped prevent Negroes, as one astute foreign observer put it, "from forming too great opinions of themselves," the underlying reason for their passage was that these mixtures were "disagreeable" to white men. Probably it was this feeling which prompted the prominent Boston merchant, James Bowdoin, to ship one of his Negroes to the West Indies in exchange for produce or another Negro boy, explaining that "my Man Caesar has been engaged in an amour with some of the white ladies of the Town." When Mrs. Anne Grant recalled her early years in the colony of New York she daintily reported that the citizens of Albany pos-sessed a particular "moral delicacy" on one point: "they were from infancy in habits of familiarity with these humble friends [the Ne-groes], yet being early taught that nature had placed between them a barrier, which it was in a high degree criminal and disgraceful to pass, they considered a mixture of such distinct races with abhor-rence, as a violation of her laws."

While the "laws" of nature seem to have appeared in abundant clarity in Albany, New York, they were very dimly perceived in Charleston, South Carolina, where white persons were surrounded by so many more "humble friends." On the face of things it seems paradoxical that the one region on the continent which had become demographically most like a new Guinea should have been the one in which white men seemed least anxious about interracial sexual activity. While permanent unions between persons of the two races normally were quiet or secretive affairs elsewhere on the continent, in South Carolina and particularly in Charleston they were not. It was the only city worthy of the name in the plantation colonies. It was an elegant, gay, extravagant city, where men took advantage of certain of their opportunities in more overt, more relaxed, and probably more enterprising fashion than in the colonies to the northward. They possessed an abundance of Negro women. The result may best be described in the words of two travelers from different backgrounds. As young Josiah Quincy of Boston reported on his tour through North and South Carolina, "The enjoyment of a negro or mulatto woman is spoken of as quite a common thing: no reluctance, delicacy or shame is made about the matter." A visiting merchant from Jamaica, where the atmosphere surrounding interracial sex was so utterly different from New England, wrote from Charleston in 1773, "I know of but one Gentleman who professedly keeps a Mulatto Mistress and he is very much pointed at: There are swarms of Negroes about the Town and many Mulattoes, and by the Dress of the Girls, who mostly imitate their Mistresses, I have no doubt of their Conversations with the whites, but they are carried on with more privacy than in our W. India Islands." (Josiah Quincy would scarcely have appreciated the niceness of the distinction.) "As I travell'd further North," the Jamaican visitor continued, concerning his trip from Charleston to North Carolina, "there were fewer Negroes about the Houses, and these taken less notice of, and before I finish'd my Journey North, I found an empty House, the late Tenant of which had been oblig'd by the Church Wardens to decamp on Account of his having kept a Black Woman. Dont suppose Fornication is out of Fashion here," he added reassuringly about North Carolina, "more than in other Places, No! the difference only is, that the White Girls monopolize it."

Here was an important regional difference in social "fashion." Charleston was the only English city on the continent where it was at all possible to jest publicly concerning miscegenation. In 1732 the *South-Carolina Gazette* published a verse which touched off a round robin on the subject.

> The CAMELEON LOVER
> *If what the* Curious *have observ'd be true,*
> *That the* Cameleon *will assume the* Hue
> *Of all the Objects that approach its* Touch;
> *No Wonder then, that the* Amours *of such*
> *Whose* Taste *betrays them to a close Embrace*
> *With the* dark *Beauties of the* Sable *Race*
> *(Stain'd with the Tincture of the* Sooty *Sin,)*
> *Imbibe the* Blackness *of their* Charmer's *Skin.*

. . . Four years later the paper published some frank advice to the bachelors and widowers of Charleston ostensibly from some ladies newly arrived from Bermuda: "that if they are in a Strait for Women, to wait for the next Shipping from the Coast of Guinny. Those African Ladies are of a strong, robust Constitution: not easily jaded out, able to serve them by Night as well as Day. When they are Sick, they are not costly, when dead, their funeral Charges are but *viz* an old Matt, one Bottle Rum, and a lb. Sugar[.] The cheapness of a Commo-di-ty becomes more taking when it fully Answers the end, or T——l." . . .

If these contributions to the *South-Carolina Gazette* were a trifle raw by the standards of a modern family newspaper, they reflected more than eighteenth-century literary frankness about sex. Newspapers elsewhere on the continent did not publish similar discussions of interracial sex, though everywhere (including Boston) they published some none-too-delicate pieces concerning sexual matters. Only in Charleston was it possible to debate publicly, "Is sex with Negroes right?" In other colonies the topic was not looked upon as being open. . . .

For white women the situation was different, and here again the Charleston area seems to have been characterized by attitudes somewhere mid-way between those of the West Indies and further north. In the islands, where English settlers were most thoroughly committed to a Negro slave society and where strenuous attempts to attract more white settlers had been unavailing, white women were, quite literally, the repositories of white civilization. White men tended to place them protectively upon a pedestal and then run off to gratify their passions elsewhere. For their part white women, though they might propagate children, inevitably held themselves aloof from the world of lust and passion, a world which reeked of infidelity and Negro slaves. Under no circumstances would they have attempted, any more than they would have been allowed, to clamber down from their pedestal to seek pleasures of their own across the racial line. In fact white women in the West Indies tended to adhere rigidly to the double sexual standard which characterized English sexual mores and to refrain more than in the continental colonies from infidelity with white men. The oppressive presence of slavery itself tended to inhibit the white woman's capacity for emotional, sexual, and intellectual commitment. She served principally an ornamentive function, for everything resembling work was done by Negro slaves. Visitors to the islands were almost universally agreed in describing her life as one of indolence and lassitude, though some were impressed by a formal, superficial gaiety. Her choices were to withdraw from the world or to create an unreal one of her own. She withdrew from the colored race and, perhaps not entirely because of prevailing notions about health, scrupulously shielded her face from the darkening effects of the tropic sun. A tanned skin implied an affinity which she had to deny.

The white women of the Charleston area were less tightly hemmed in. Nevertheless, they rarely if ever established liaisons with Negro men, as happened in the South Carolina back country. . . . The dissipation of the white gentleman was as much a tragedy for his white lady as for him. A biracial environment warped her affective life in two directions at once, for she was made to feel that sensual involvement with the opposite sex burned bright and hot with unquenchable passion and at the same time that any such involvement was utterly repulsive. Accordingly . . . she approached her prospective legitimate sexual partners as if she were picking up a live coal in one hand and a dead rat in the other.

If women were particularly affected by the situation in South Carolina, white persons of both sexes in *all* the English colonies were affected in a more general way by the tensions involved in miscegenation. Though these tensions operated in white men rather differently than in white women, it seems almost self-evident that the emergent attitudes toward Negroes possessed a unity which transcended differences between the two sexes. Put another way, out of a pattern of interracial sexual relationships which normally placed white men and white women in very different roles, there arose a common core of belief and mythology concerning the Negro which belonged to neither sex but to white American culture as a whole. The emergence of common beliefs out of divergent experiences was of course principally a function of the homogenizing effect of culture upon individual experience, but it is important to bear in mind that the functional significance of beliefs about the Negro may have been very different for white women than for white men even when the beliefs themselves were identical. Since the English and colonial American cultures were dominated by males, however, sexually oriented beliefs about the Negro in America derived principally from the psychological needs of men and were to a considerable extent shaped by specifically masculine modes of thought and behavior. This is not to say that American attitudes toward the Negro were *male* attitudes but merely that when one talks about *American* attitudes toward anything (the frontier, the city, money, freedom, the Negro) one is using a shorthand for attitudes common to both sexes but predominantly male in genesis and tone.

As for these ideas or beliefs about the Negro, many seem startlingly modern. Least surprising, perhaps, was the common assumption that Negro women were especially passionate, an idea which found literary or at least literate expression especially in the *South-Carolina Gazette* and in West Indian books. The Negro woman was the sunkissed embodiment of ardency:

> *Next comes a warmer race, from sable sprung,*
> *To love each thought, to lust each nerve is strung;*
> *The Samboe dark, and the Mullattoe brown,*
> *The Mestize fair, the well-limb'd Quaderoon,*
> *And jetty Afric, from no spurious sire,*
> *Warm as her soil, and as her sun—on fire.*
> *These sooty dames, well vers'd in Venus' school,*
> *Make love an art, and boast they kiss by rule.*

If such amiable assessments could find their way into public print, one can imagine what tavern bantering must have been like. There may well have been, of course, objective basis in fact for this assessment of Negro women, for just as the white woman's experience tended to inhibit sexual expression, so the Negro woman's very different situation may have encouraged it. Yet plainly white men were doing more than reporting pleasant facts. For by calling the Negro woman passionate they were offering the best possible justification for their own passions. Not only did the Negro woman's warmth constitute a logical explanation for the white man's infidelity, but, much more important, it helped shift responsibility from himself to her. If she was *that* lascivious—well, a man could scarcely be blamed for succumbing against overwhelming odds. Further reinforcement for this picture of the Negro woman came from the ancient association of hot climates with sexual activity, a tradition which persists today despite the introduction of central heating. Operating less strongly in the same direction was the old equation of barbarism with sexual abandonment: Negro women seemed more natural and were sometimes described, for instance, as giving birth more easily than white women.

Further Reading

Professor Jordan's study of the dynamics of interracial sex before 1812 is based upon primary sources not readily available to the undergraduate. The author does make some use of Edward B. Reuter's *The Mulatto in the United States* (Boston, 1918), but otherwise the student must tease material out of more accessible works that embrace a broad theme and/or time period, such as E. Franklin Frazier, *The Negro Family in the United States* (Chicago, 1939); B. A. Botkin (ed.), *Lay My Burden Down: A Folk History of Slavery* (Chicago, 1945); Angela Davis, "Reflections on the Black Woman's Role in the Community of Slaves," *Black Scholar* (December, 1971), pp. 3–15; and Robert Staples (ed.), *The Black Family: Essays and Studies* (Belmont, Calif., 1971). Keen analyses of interracial sex from the Southern white woman's point of view are found in Mary Boykin Chesnut's *A Diary From Dixie,* edited by Ben A. William (Boston, 1949); and Lillian Smith's *Killers of the Dream* (New York, 1949). The best general source for studying the black woman is Gerda Lerner's *Black Women in White America: A Documentary History* (New York, 1972), which contains a comprehensive selection of primary sources, as well as "Bibliographical Notes" (pp. 615–629) that provide the student with discussion of a variety of topical themes, such as black women and education, racism, slavery and abolition. For a brief introduction to the subject, see Johnneta B. Cole, "Black Women in America: An Annotated Bibliography," *Black Scholar* (December, 1971), pp. 42–53.

Walter O'Meara
SEX ON THE AMERICAN INDIAN FRONTIER

Walter O'Meara, like Ann Stanford, is not a professionally trained historian, but a writer. In the following selection the author provides the reader with a description of Indian women's life-styles and their place within Indian culture on the colonial American frontier. O'Meara contends that one must take care not to reduce Indian womanhood to a stereotype. Although Indian women were usually subordinated to male authority, their place within Indian culture varied dramatically from one tribe to another, with their influence often depending upon the importance given their economic function. At the same time, there were features of their life-styles that were common to most, especially when measured against white women's modes of behavior. Characteristically, being free from moralistic tenets regarding sexual conduct, Indian women were less inhibited than their white sisters and more flexible in their attitude toward marriage. Polygamous marriages were widespread and divorce not unusual. Still, most Indian women were devoted to their men and tried to embrace virtues similar to those expected of Sioux women: bravery, generosity, truthfulness and childbearing.

. . . The cooking, sewing, child rearing, and housekeeping—was only a small part of an Indian woman's tasks. She also gathered wild berries and fruits, root vegetables, and herbs. She helped to harvest the wild rice and boil down the sap of the sugar maple. She dried the surplus meat her husband brought in from the buffalo hunt—or, more likely, left on the spot for her to bring in. She tanned the hides and from them fashioned lodge covers. She made the tipi, set it up, and took it down when the encampment moved on. She cut wood and brought it to the lodge fire. On the move, she packed the horses, and when a new campsite was reached, "she unpacks the animals, pitches the lodge, makes the beds, brings food and water, and does everything that is to be done, and when her husband returns from the hunt, is ready to take and unsaddle his horse."

Her assigned tasks conformed to her tribe's economic environment. Among the agricultural Indians such as the Huron, the women were, as Pierre François Xavier de Charlevoix noted, "charged with the culture of the fields"—that is, they planted and hoed the maize,

Selectively edited from Chapter 3 of Part 1 of *Daughters of the Country: The Women of the Fur Traders and Mountain Men,* © 1968 by Walter O'Meara. Reprinted by permission of Harcourt Brace Jovanovich, Inc. Footnotes omitted.

pumpkins, and beans, harvested them, and processed them for winter storage. The women of the canoe Indians plied their own paddles and carried their share on the backbreaking portages. Captain William Clark was astonished to find a Chinook woman shouldering a load that was "almost as much as a man could lift, and above one hundred pounds in weight." . . .

Women as a rule accompanied war parties only as drudges and prostitutes, but there were individual cases of females taking the war road on their own and becoming famous as warriors. At La Pointe, a young Ojibway girl joined the fighting men of her tribe, raised the scalp of a wounded Sioux, and won great acclaim when she returned from battle. And Denig tells of a Crow girl captive, "tolerably good-looking," who not only became a full-fledged brave but rose to the rank of a chief. She led raids against the Blackfoot, killed and scalped with her own hands—and, in keeping with her character of a warrior, married three women according to the rites of her tribe. . . .

Although it was only in desperate circumstances that Indian women joined their men in battle—as the Aricara women did, "fighting like demons" against Colonel Leavenworth's troops—they were expected to perform special duties in time of war. The Apache women formed a reserve corps which rounded up horses while the men attacked, and by their numbers thus made the war party look larger and more formidable than it actually was. Women, as in all warrior societies, were skilled in treating the wounded after battle. And the Pueblo Indians sent their girls "to excite the Spaniards to lewdness," in preparation for a surprise night attack.

All in all, it can be seen that the Indian woman led a rather active life. Even when she grew too old to cut and fetch firewood, hoe corn, or carry heavy loads, she was set to weaving mats, taking care of the children, disciplining the dogs, and performing other "light" tasks about the lodge. . . .

In most tribes a fair division of labor seems to have obtained, and perhaps the Indian woman spent no more time complaining of her lot than the modern suburban housewife does of hers. She was sure, at least, of her place in the domestic economy, and plagued by no sense of unfulfillment, nor any confusion about her role in society. Even in the pages of the most cynical traders, we frequently catch glimpses of her gay and happy at her work. Walter McClintock,

FIGURE 2. The native American woman's status varied from tribe to tribe with her influence often depending on the importance given to her economic function. *(Historical Pictures Service, Chicago)*

who lived with the Indians and knew them well, says: "Women considered it a disgrace for men to do any of their work—put up lodges, tan skins, cook food at home or look after provisions; all this was a woman's work in which they were trained from childhood, and they resented any interference from the men." . . .

Anthropologists speculate that the abysmal status of Indian women in some tribes may have been an expression of innate hostility between the sexes. Women were regarded as dangerous adversaries, foes to be conquered and humiliated. For this reason they were hedged about with innumerable taboos. They must spend their menstrual periods alone in tiny segregation huts. They must prepare the meals but eat apart from the men. They must dance by themselves and never touch a warrior's hunting or fighting gear. In some tribes they were thrown on their husband's funeral pyre, then hauled off by friends, then thrown on again, and so on, until dreadfully burned and insensible. (Wootton says the Ute sometimes burned wives with their dead husbands.) In other tribes, a widow was condemned to carry her husband's ashes about with her for two or three years and remain a slave to his nearest kin. And in almost all Indian societies a certain amount of mutilation and disfigurement was expected of women as part of their mourning for lost mates.

Apart from the taboos, there were other tribal expressions of sexual hostility and contempt: the Sioux custom, for example, of the young men counting coup for coitus, and the enforced use of chastity belts.

All this, it has been suggested, was rooted in the male's "unresolved masculine fear" that his physical powers would be lowered by sustained sexual intercourse—a view which was advanced by Lahontan at a very early date—and certainly a worrisome possibility to people whose existence depended on the physical fitness of the men.

As in most other aspects of Indian life, a woman's status varied from one tribe to another. Much depended on her importance in the economy. Where the men were the breadwinners, Ross Cox points out, the women were condemned to a life of drudgery; where the women were important as root-gatherers, "they assume an air of liberty and independence." Captain Meriwether Lewis agrees with Cox:

> The importance of the female in savage life, has no necessary relation to the virtues of the men, but is regulated wholly by their capacity to be useful. . . . Where the woman can aid in procuring subsistence for the tribe, they are treated with more equality, and their importance is proportioned to the share which they take in that labor; while in countries where subsistence is chiefly procured by the exertions of the men, the women are considered and treated as burdens.

*   *   *

To observe womanhood at its most abject, we must visit the northern tribes, such as the Chipewyan of the Lake Athabasca region. It would be hard to imagine a degree of degradation lower than the one reflected in a report from Fort Wedderburn by Sir George

Simpson, governor of the Hudson's Bay Company: "The Bustard's wife died this morning, or more properly speaking a termination was put to her sufferings as she was actually buried before the vital spark was extinguished." So little were the women of the Chipewyan valued, and so harshly were they treated, that David Thompson tells us:

> This hard usage makes women scarce among them, and by the time a girl is twelve years of age she is given as a Wife to a man twice her age. . . . The hardships the Women suffer, induce them, too often to let the female infants die, as soon as born; and they look upon it as an act of kindness to them. And when any of us spoke to a women who had thus acted, the common answer was: "She wished her mother had done the same to herself."

The men of the Cree, the Arctic explorer Sir John Franklin wrote, kept up a curious pretense of despising their womenfolk while treating them well; they surrounded them with many taboo reminders of their inferiority and grew furious with a white man who so far forgot himself as to treat an Indian wife tenderly.

But it was not only among the bleak northern tribes that women were considered inferior, if indeed human at all, and were saddled to boot with a vague primitive onus of harboring something innately evil. Even the advanced Plains nations were something less than chivalrous. The Sioux, as we have seen, despite the romanticizing indulged in by the admirers of that great people, had little basic respect for their women. The Mandan women, although "beautiful and modest," were gladly sold for a couple of horses and a gun; and Catlin relates that the men of the tribe were outraged when he painted their women's portraits—thus giving squaws an importance equal to that of warriors. . . .

Like many another trader, Daniel Harmon drew some general conclusions about the Indian's treatment of his women, and they are not very favorable. "All the Indians," he said, "consider women as far inferior in every respect, to men; and among many tribes, they treat their wives much as they do their dogs. The men chastise their wives frequently, with an axe, or with a large club; and in the presence of their husbands, the women dare not look a person in the face." Having thus generalized, however, Harmon proceeds to make some important exceptions:

Among the Sauteaux [an Ojibway band], Crees, Muscagoes, and As-
siniboins, however, the women are treated with more gentleness and
respect. The husband shares the labor with his wife; and the women
govern everything in their tents, so that the husband presumes not to
dispose of the most trifling article, without the consent of his wife. Among
them the husband kills animals and generally brings the meat to his tent,
where his wife prepares it for drying, and melts down the fat. She also
generally does the cooking; not, however, without the occasional as-
sistance of her husband.

He also assisted her, Harmon tells us, in taking care of the children, and if his wife was too heavily laden on the march, he even
went so far as to take one of the children on his back.

It seems to have been true that in some tribes wives enjoyed a
respect and influence comparable to that of modern American
women. The most frequently quoted example, of course, is that of
the Iroquois. This great federation of powerful tribes possessed the
most highly organized social and political life of any Indian nation,
and its core was the "fireside," consisting of the mother and all her
children. The nation was composed of clans, the clans of *ohwachira,*
and the *ohwachira* of all the descendants of a particular woman.
From generation to generation, the eldest daughters succeeded to
leadership of the *ohwachira,* and all basic authority stemmed from
the *ohwachira* and the women who headed them. Thus, in theory at
least, Iroquois women were the dominant sex.

In reality, however, not even the Iroquois society was a true
matriarchy. Descent, to be sure, was traced through the mother, and
nominal leadership was in the hands of the *ohwachira,* but most of
the Iroquois woman's authority was symbolic. As Charlevoix pointed
out, there was much pretense, much form, but little substance.

Still, the women of the Five Nations did take part to a remarkable
extent in a male-oriented culture. Girls were as fondly and permis-
sively treated as boys. Women accepted a fair share of labor, but
were not burdened. And, although not ruling in a true "matriarchal"
sense, they could and did exert a strong influence on the decisions
of the sachems in council. Even today, it has been pointed out,
Iroquois women are remarkably resolute and self-reliant, and seem
to be more secure in their feminine role than their masculine counterparts.

The western Pueblo Indians and the Navajo also inherited through the mother; and the women, Cabeza de Vaca noted at a very early date, were "treated with more decorum than in any part of the Indies we had visited." Among the Natchez, the chief's nearest female relative (through whom succession to the "throne" was traced) was accorded great honor but had no real authority in council. She did, however, possess considerable power; and, according to Charlevoix, when she pointed at one of her people and said, "Go, rid me of this dog," she was taken quite literally. Those she passed on the road were, indeed, required to howl like dogs.

In various other tribes women were accorded at least a symbolic authority in such matters as arranging marriages. An Ojibway woman could gain full membership in the Midewiwin, her people's Grand Medicine society. In many tribes women were given power of life or death over prisoners of war. Sometimes, as we have seen, a woman even became a chief; but although a girl might dream of fighting with the war bands and taking scalps, she rarely succeeded in escaping from the reality of male domination in a warrior society. . . .

The Indians considered marriage strictly a private affair, an agreement between a man and a woman to live with each other; and the event was usually marked by nothing more ritualistic than the young couple's going to bed together. Some tribes, such as the Iroquois, the Huron, and the ceremony-loving peoples of the Pacific Coast, asked friends and neighbors in for a little dancing and drinking, but for the most part Indians reserved their more elaborate rites for burying and name-giving. A wedding had no overtones of sanctification or religious import.

The events leading up to marriage, however, might have their interesting aspects. The Athabascan Indians, for example, often wrestled for wives; and a strong man might collect half a dozen young and good-looking girls, while a weakling had to content himself with a tribal reject or no wife at all. The Shoshoni, following an ancient primitive ritual of chase and capture, ran a foot race for a mate, giving the girl a head start and pursuing her with a lasso; if he caught her, she was "tied to him for life." The Ute Indians had a still simpler system: the man seated himself on a log outside the village and waited for the girl to come and sit down beside him; the courtship was then considered ended, and married life began without more ado. An Assiniboin warrior tied two horses outside the girl's lodge, then another, then another, until she gave in or sent him packing.

Sometimes, it would seem, the girl boldly took the initiative. When she came of age, she might spread her blanket in front of the family tipi and invite suitors to share it with her. Young men lined up—with members of the family, and even other villagers, passing by—to pay her court.

This matter of sharing a blanket was, in one form or another, a basic aspect of Indian courtship. It was an outgrowth, perhaps, of the custom of the man's lying down at night outside the tipi and reaching in to where the object of his desire was sleeping. What ensued, anthropologists inform us, went a good way beyond a mere tugging at the blankets, with the outcome more than likely to lead to matrimony.

Blanket-sharing was observed and reported on by Lahontan, Peter Pond, Jonathan Carver, Alexander Henry, and other early commentators on Indian customs. It involved a stealthy nocturnal visit to the girl's lodge after a careful daytime reconnaissance of her sleeping place. The procedure, described by the American trader Peter Pond in his original orthography, was as follows:

> When all the famaley are quiet and perhaps a sleep he slids soffely into that [place] and seat himself down by her side. Preasantlay he will begin to lift her blanket in a soft maner. Perhaps she may twich it out of his hand with a sort of sie and snore to gather but this is no killing matter. He seats awhile and makes a second atempt. She may perhaps hold the blankeat down slitely. At lengh she turns over with a sith and quits hold of the blanket.

Henry describes a variant of this mode of courtship. The young man comes into the tipi with a splinter of wood, which he lights in the embers of the lodge fire. When he has found the young woman by its light, he whispers to her—after perhaps having had to awaken her—and if successful takes part of her mat. "I consider this practice," Henry adds, "as precisely similar to the bundling of New England and other countries; and to say the least, is not more licentious." The young man, Henry makes clear, brought his own blanket. . . .

On the whole, marriage among the Indians was a casual matter and courtship little hampered by subtle conventions. A youth might begin by gently pelting his sweetheart with bits of earth, snowballs, small sticks, or anything else at hand; if she returned the compliment, he would be emboldened to engage her in some rather ribald repartee, and marriage followed not long after. Or perhaps he would throw a deer's carcass down in front of the girl's lodge, and keep this up until her father demanded to know what his intentions were. An Apache warrior simply staked his horse in front of the girl's lodge at night; if she took the horse within four days, fed and watered it, and returned it to the hopeful owner, everything was settled. It does not seem that the historic phenomenon we call romantic love was an especially complicating factor in most cases. . . .

Yet Indian lore and myth are rich in love stories. Callow youths mooned about the encampments playing melancholy music to their mistresses on courting flutes. Indian girls not infrequently resorted to love potions and charms, such as figurines carved from wood representing a man and a woman, and tied together face to face with a hair from the head of the desired one. The seeds of the false gromwell (*Onosmodium hispidissimum*) were supposed to have "great attractive power." . . .

Thus, while an Indian marriage did involve such practical details as trading between parents, preliminary gift-giving, and payment of a bride-price, the element of romance was not always lacking. Young people could usually contrive to make their own choice of mates; and not infrequently elopements frustrated the best-laid plans of scheming parents. In some tribes, however, brides were bestowed at ages as early as six or seven—to make sure of their virginity, the trader Duncan Cameron cynically surmised.

The Huron, Samuel de Champlain noted in his *Voyages,* carried the Indians' casual attitude toward marriage to its logical conclusion: trial marriage. The customary presents were exchanged, the young couple lived together for a week or two, and if it did not work out, each felt free to try again with another mate. The whole experiment was simplified by the fact that, among the Huron, a girl was under no chastity requirements before marriage; although, Champlain says, "after marriage the women were chaste and their husbands generally jealous." . . .

Indian marriages could fall apart as easily as they were put together. Either husband or wife commonly felt free to get rid of a spouse for the lightest of reasons. . . .

. . . Of the Chipewyan, for example, Hearne wrote: "The Ceremony [of divorce] . . . consists of neither more nor less than a good drubbing and turning the woman out of doors, telling her to go to her paramour or relations, according to the nature of her crime." All a Sioux husband had to do was beat the drum and announce that he had thrown out his woman; not infrequently, Kurz remarks, without distressing "the little wife" too much, since she was tired of her mate anyhow.

So divorce was a two-way street in Indian society, with the woman as free as the man to pack up and leave. In most tribes she had only to pile her husband's personal gear in front of their lodge—public notice that she intended to go her way without him. . . .

In the eighteenth century, the women of the Shawnee amazed colonial army officers with a mass divorce of their husbands and the selection of new mates more to their liking. On this memorable occasion, they opened festivities with a proclamation that all marriages were dissolved. Then followed a three-day feast, during which the women sang, "I am not afraid of my husband, I will choose what man I please." On the third day, a hundred men danced past the women, each of whom chose the one she wanted and danced with him. "After which," Colonel Mercer, an eye-witness, wrote to Christopher Gist, "the dance ended, and they all retired to consummate." . . .

. . . Polygamy, among the Indians, was imposed by economic necessity and by an excess of women in a warring society. It was part of the pattern of survival, and as advantageous to wives as to husbands. "Polygamy among the Indians is no indication of sensuality," Kurz explained, "but simply shows their system of labor." An extra wife, in other words, was an extra "hand."

The more successful an Indian was as a hunter, the more wives he needed to prepare skins, dry meat, and so on. And, with the coming of the white trader, the stepped-up demand for pelts increased the need. This was especially true among the Plains Indians, where the bison economy made the support of large polygamous families possible. It was less true of the forest Indians, where a man often found it difficult to support even one wife and her offspring. Hence polygamy, while not unknown, was less prevalent among such tribes as the Ojibway and Woods Cree.

The economic basis for plural marriage was a fortunate circumstance for older and less attractive women. A man did not refuse a woman because she was no longer young or beautiful; if she was willing and able to work, she had a place in the lodge. "Of course," Kurz says, "a man aims to have always apart a dainty one for his own private pleasure, but the others are for the most part working women —old maids or widows—who are glad to belong to a family."

Aside from economic reasons, an Indian often took on additional wives from a sense of social responsibility, or for political motives. It was quite common for a man to marry his dead brother's wife or wives. Sisters were often married collectively; and some tribes recognized a man's right to all the younger sisters of his bride, or even his obligation to support them. Where wife-lending and wife-swapping were practiced extensively, it was necessary for important men to have a supply of wives—preferably young and good-looking —in order to extend the hospitality their position in society required. As a demand for more wives arose, the age of brides tended to decrease, and it was customary for all wives lower in the scale than number 3 or number 4 to be known as "slave wives," kept chiefly for lending purposes.

One might suppose it difficult to maintain harmonious relations between half a dozen women, or even fewer, in the same lodge. But Indian wives, as a matter of fact, seem seldom to have quarreled or engaged in jealous feuds. . . . The first wife was in charge, and her authority was accepted by the others, who were often her sisters. A husband with a roving eye was even likely to find his wives united on keeping him in line.

Polygamy tended to lighten the burden of the Indian woman, and to provide a certain security for her in old age. She was not abandoned by her husband, since he felt free to take a younger wife or two while keeping the old ones. And most Indian wives seem to have enjoyed the sociability of the polygamous lodge, especially if the other wives were her sisters.

Even under such conditions of drudgery, tyrannical domination, summary divorce, and the husband-sharing of a polygamous marriage, the Indian wife was not invariably discontented with her role. If the journals of the traders are sprinkled with recitals of domestic misery, they are also lightened occasionally with little stories of wifely devotion and the love of Indian husbands for their lodge mates. . . .

The four female virtues, the Sioux held, were bravery, generosity, truthfulness, and childbearing. The feminine goal was "to be loving, industrious, generous, and kind to all men and animals." That many Indian wives and mothers sought and possessed these virtues is well attested by the loyalty and devotion of their men. "The Spokane women," Ross Cox says, "are good wives and most affectionate mothers. . . . The women of the Flatheads are excellent wives and mothers . . . and we have never heard of one of them proving unfaithful to her husband." Over and over, the fort journals and wilderness diaries pause to pay similar tribute to the loyalty, courage, and devotion of the Indian woman. . . .

Further Reading

As is the case with the subject of black women, there are almost no scholarly studies that deal with Indian women except in twentieth-century American life. For the most part observations about Indian women must be gleaned either from secondary material that deals with a particular tribe, or from primary sources, especially those of white traders and explorers. Walter O'Meara makes use of a number of the latter materials, such as George Catlin, *North American Indians, Being Letters and Notes on Their Manners, Customs, and Conditions* (2 vols., Edinburgh, 1926); Daniel W. Harmon, *A Journal of Voyages and Travels in the Interior of North America,* edited by Daniel Haskell (Andover, 1820); Samuel Hearne, *A Journey from Prince of Wales' Fort in Hudson's Bay . . . ,* edited by J. B. Tyrrell (Toronto, 1911); and Alexander Mackenzie, *Voyages from Montreal . . . through the Continent of North America . . . in the Years 1789 and 1793 . . . ,* edited by John W. Garvin (Toronto, 1927). Also helpful in studying Indian women are the publications of the Bureau of American Ethnology, Washington, D.C.: Frances Densmore, "Chippewa Customs," *Bulletin* 86 (1929); Rudolph F. Kurz, "Journal of . . . ," trans. by Myrtis Jarrell and edited by J. N. B. Hewitt, *Bulletin* 115 (1937); and Martha C. Randle, "Iroquois Women Then and Now," *Bulletin* 149 (1951). Two more-recent books should be noted as well: Mari Sandoz, *Love Songs to the Plains* (New York, 1961); and Royal B. Hassrick, *The Sioux: Life and Customs of a Warrior Society* (Norman, 1964).

III NINETEENTH-CENTURY AMERICA

Contemporary Observations

The next three selections make clear that there was some sharp difference of opinion regarding the nature of the woman's status in nineteenth-century America. French observer Alexis de Tocqueville, for example, noted that Protestantism/democracy invested woman with a high degree of equality and freedom. Compared with her European sisters she enjoyed a marked amount of independence; that is, until she married. Marriage, according to de Tocqueville, was a watershed in her life, as she gave up her former freedom willingly in order to fulfill her womanly nature. Harriet Martineau, an English visitor in her mid-thirties, saw things differently. She was quite troubled by what "democratic principles" had wrought—woman's intellect was confined, her health ruined, and her weakness cultivated by male conventional wisdom. Woman was being "bought off" by rhetoric that praised womanhood, and intimidated by warnings that her feminine nature would be compromised if she pursued activities outside of her sphere. For Martineau, democracy ironically was contributing to the subjugation of woman. While Catharine Beecher and her sister, Harriet Beecher Stowe, agreed with Martineau that all was not well with the American lady, they differed with her as to the cause. For woman to improve her lot, she must legitimize her domestic function, not seek alternatives to it by pursuing "peculiarly masculine" activities. Since womanhood was based upon motherhood and wifedom, domestic reformers such as Beecher and Stowe sought to encourage woman to approach her God-given role with pride, knowledge and enthusiasm.

Alexis de Tocqueville
ON AMERICAN MAIDENS AND WIVES
(1835)

Education of Young Women in the United States

. . . Amongst almost all Protestant nations young women are far
more the mistresses of their own actions than they are in Catholic
countries. This independence is still greater in Protestant countries,
like England, which have retained or acquired the right of self-
government; the spirit of freedom is then infused into the domestic
circle by political habits and by religious opinions. In the United
States the doctrines of Protestantism are combined with great political freedom and a most democratic state of society; and nowhere
are young women surrendered so early or so completely to their
own guidance. Long before an American girl arrives at the age of
marriage, her emancipation from maternal control begins; she has
scarcely ceased to be a child when she already thinks for herself,
speaks with freedom, and acts on her own impulse. The great scene
of the world is constantly open to her view; far from seeking con-
cealment, it is every day disclosed to her more completely, and she
is taught to survey it with a firm and calm gaze. Thus the vices and
dangers of society are early revealed to her; as she sees them
clearly, she views them without illusions, and braves them without
fear; for she is full of reliance on her own strength, and her reliance
seems to be shared by all who are about her. An American girl
scarcely ever displays that virginal bloom in the midst of young
desires, or that innocent and ingenuous grace which usually attends
the European woman in the transition from girlhood to youth. It is
rarely that an American woman at any age displays childish timidity
or ignorance. Like the young women of Europe, she seeks to please,
but she knows precisely the cost of pleasing. If she does not abandon
herself to evil, at least she knows that it exists; and she is remarkable
rather for purity of manners than for chastity of mind. I have been
frequently surprised, and almost frightened, at the singular address
and happy boldness with which young women in America contrive to
manage their thoughts and their language amidst all the difficulties

From *Democracy in America*, trans. Henry Reeve (rev. ed.; New York, 1900), Vol. II.

of stimulating conversation; a philosopher would have stumbled at every step along the narrow path which they trod without accidents and without effort. It is easy indeed to perceive that, even amidst the independence of early youth, an American woman is always mistress of herself; she indulges in all permitted pleasures, without yielding herself up to any of them; and her reason never allows the reins of self-guidance to drop, though it often seems to hold them loosely. . . .

The Young Woman in the Character of a Wife

In America the independence of woman is irrecoverably lost in the bonds of matrimony: if an unmarried woman is less constrained there than elsewhere, a wife is subjected to stricter obligations. The former makes her father's house an abode of freedom and of pleasure; the latter lives in the home of her husband as if it were a cloister. Yet these two different conditions of life are perhaps not so contrary as may be supposed, and it is natural that the American women should pass through the one to arrive at the other.

Religious peoples and trading nations entertain peculiarly serious notions of marriage: the former consider the regularity of woman's life as the best pledge and most certain sign of the purity of her morals; the latter regard it as the highest security for the order and prosperity of the household. The Americans are at the same time a puritanical people and a commercial nation: their religious opinions, as well as their trading habits, consequently lead them to require much abnegation on the part of woman, and a constant sacrifice of her pleasures to her duties which is seldom demanded of her in Europe. Thus in the United States the inexorable opinion of the public carefully circumscribes woman within the narrow circle of domestic interests and duties, and forbids her to step beyond it.

Upon her entrance into the world a young American woman finds these notions firmly established; she sees the rules which are derived from them; she is not slow to perceive that she cannot depart for an instant from the established usages of her contemporaries, without putting in jeopardy her peace of mind, her honor, nay even her social existence; and she finds the energy required for such an act of submission in the firmness of her understanding and in the virile habits which her education has given her. It may be said that she has learned by the use of her independence to surrender it without a struggle and without a murmur when the time comes for making the sacrifice. But no American woman falls into the toils of matrimony as into a snare held out to her simplicity and ignorance. She has been taught beforehand what is expected of her, and voluntarily and freely does she enter upon this engagement. She supports her new condition with courage, because she chose it. As in America paternal discipline is very relaxed and the conjugal tie very strict, a young woman does not contract the latter without considerable circumspection and apprehension. Precocious marriages are rare. Thus American women do not marry until their understandings are exercised and ripened; whereas in other countries most women generally only begin to exercise and to ripen their understandings after marriage.

I by no means suppose, however, that the great change which takes place in all the habits of women in the United States, as soon as they are married, ought solely to be attributed to the constraint of public opinion: it is frequently imposed upon themselves by the sole effort of their own will. When the time for choosing a husband is arrived, that cold and stern reasoning power which has been educated and invigorated by the free observation of the world, teaches an American woman that a spirit of levity and independence in the bonds of marriage is a constant subject of annoyance, not of pleasure; it tells her that the amusements of the girl cannot become the recreations of the wife, and that the sources of a married woman's happiness are in the home of her husband. As she clearly discerns beforehand the only road which can lead to domestic happiness, she enters upon it at once, and follows it to the end without seeking to turn back. . . .

How the Americans Understand the Equality of the Sexes

. . . There are people in Europe who, confounding together the different characteristics of the sexes, would make of man and woman beings not only equal but alike. They would give to both the same functions, impose on both the same duties, and grant to both the same rights; they would mix them in all things—their occupations, their pleasures, their business. It may readily be conceived, that by thus attempting to make one sex equal to the other, both are degraded; and from so preposterous a medley of the works of nature nothing could ever result but weak men and disorderly women.

It is not thus that the Americans understand that species of democratic equality which may be established between the sexes. They admit, that as nature has appointed such wide differences between the physical and moral constitution of man and woman, her manifest design was to give a distinct employment to their various faculties; and they hold that improvement does not consist in making beings so dissimilar do pretty nearly the same things, but in getting each of them to fulfill their respective tasks in the best possible manner. The Americans have applied to the sexes the great principle of political economy which governs the manufactures of our age, by carefully dividing the duties of man from those of woman, in order that the great work of society may be the better carried on.

In no country has such constant care been taken as in America to trace two clearly distinct lines of action for the two sexes, and to make them keep pace one with the other, but in two pathways which are always different. American women never manage the outward concerns of the family, or conduct a business, or take a part in political life; nor are they, on the other hand, ever compelled to perform the rough labor of the fields, or to make any of those laborious exertions which demand the exertion of physical strength. No families are so poor as to form an exception to this rule. If on the one hand an American woman cannot escape from the quiet circle of domestic employments, on the other hand she is never forced to go beyond it. Hence it is that the women of America, who often exhibit a masculine strength of understanding and a manly energy, generally preserve great delicacy of personal appearance and always retain the manners of women, although they sometimes show that they have the hearts and minds of men.

Nor have the Americans ever supposed that one consequence of democratic principles is the subversion of marital power, of the confusion of the natural authorities in families. They hold that every association must have a head in order to accomplish its object, and that the natural head of the conjugal association is man. They do not therefore deny him the right of directing his partner; and they maintain, that in the smaller association of husband and wife, as well as in the great social community, the object of democracy is to

regulate and legalize the powers which are necessary, not to sub-
vert all power. This opinion is not peculiar to one sex, and contested
by the other: I never observed that the women of America consider
conjugal authority as a fortunate usurpation of their rights, nor that
they thought themselves degraded by submitting to it. It appeared to
me, on the contrary, that they attach a sort of pride to the voluntary
surrender of their own will, and make it their boast to bend themselves to the yoke, not to shake it off. Such at least is the feeling
expressed by the most virtuous of their sex; the others are silent;
and in the United States it is not the practice for a guilty wife to
clamor for the rights of women, whilst she is trampling on her holiest
duties. . . .

    . . . It is true that the Americans rarely lavish upon women those
eager attentions which are commonly paid them in Europe; but their
conduct to women always implies that they suppose them to be
virtuous and refined; and such is the respect entertained for the
moral freedom of the sex, that in the presence of a woman the most
guarded language is used, lest her ear should be offended by an
expression. In America a young unmarried woman may, alone and
without fear, undertake a long journey.

    The legislators of the United States, who have mitigated almost all
the penalties of criminal law, still make rape a capital offence, and
no crime is visited with more inexorable severity by public opinion.
This may be accounted for; as the Americans can conceive nothing
more precious than a woman's honor, and nothing which ought so
much to be respected as her independence, they hold that no
punishment is too severe for the man who deprives her of them
against her will. In France, where the same offence is visited with
far milder penalties, it is frequently difficult to get a verdict from a
jury against the prisoner. Is this a consequence of contempt of
decency or contempt of women? I cannot but believe that it is a
contempt of one and of the other.

    Thus the Americans do not think that man and woman have either
the duty or the right to perform the same offices, but they show an
equal regard for both their respective parts; and though their lot is
different, they consider both of them as beings of equal value. They
do not give to the courage of woman the same form or the same
direction as to that of man; but they never doubt her courage: and
if they hold that man and his partner ought not always to exercise

their intellect and understanding in the same manner, they at least believe the understanding of the one to be as sound as that of the other, and her intellect to be as clear. Thus, then, whilst they have allowed the social inferiority of woman to subsist, they have done all they could to raise her morally and intellectually to the level of man; and in this respect they appear to me to have excellently understood the true principle of democratic improvement. As for myself, I do not hesitate to avow that, although the women of the United States are confined within the narrow circle of domestic life, and their situation is in some respects one of extreme dependence, I have nowhere seen woman occupying a loftier position; and if I were asked, now that I am drawing to the close of this work, in which I have spoken of so many important things done by the Americans, to what the singular prosperity and growing strength of that people ought mainly to be attributed, I should reply—to the superiority of their women.

Harriet Martineau
WOMAN (1837)

If a test of civilization be sought, none can be so sure as the condition of that half of society over which the other half has power—from the exercise of the right of the strongest. Tried by this test, the American civilization appears to be of a lower order than might have been expected from some other symptoms of its social state. The Americans have, in the treatment of women, fallen below, not only their own democratic principles, but the practice of some parts of the Old World.

The unconsciousness of both parties as to the injuries suffered by women at the hands of those who hold the power is a sufficient proof of the low degree of civilization in this important particular at which they rest. While woman's intellect is confined, her morals crushed, her health ruined, her weaknesses encouraged, and her

From *Society in America* (2nd ed.; London, 1837), Vol. 3.

strength punished, she is told that her lot is cast in the paradise of women: and there is no country in the world where there is so much boasting of the "chivalrous" treatment she enjoys. That is to say— she has the best place in stage-coaches: when there are not chairs enough for everybody, the gentlemen stand: she hears oratorical flourishes on public occasions about wives and home, and apostrophes to woman: her husband's hair stands on end at the idea of her working, and he toils to indulge her with money: she has liberty to get her brain turned by religious excitements, that her attention may be diverted from morals, politics, and philosophy; and, especially, her morals are guarded by the strictest observance of propriety in her presence. In short, indulgence is given her as a substitute for justice. Her case differs from that of the slave, as to the principle, just so far as this: that the indulgence is large and universal, instead of petty and capricious. In both cases, justice is denied on no better plea than the right of the strongest. In both cases, the acquiescence of the many, and the burning discontent of the few, of the oppressed testify, the one to the actual degradation of the class, and the other to its fitness for the enjoyment of human rights. . . .

The intellect of woman is confined by an unjustifiable restriction of both methods of education—by express teaching, and by the discipline of circumstance. The former, though prior in the chronology of each individual, is a direct consequence of the latter, as regards the whole of the sex. As women have none of the objects in life for which an enlarged education is considered requisite, the education is not given. Female education in America is much what it is in England. There is a profession of some things being taught which are supposed necessary because everybody learns them. They serve to fill up time, to occupy attention harmlessly, to improve conversation, and to make women something like companions to their husbands, and able to teach their children somewhat. But what is given is, for the most part, passively received; and what is obtained is, chiefly, by means of the memory. There is rarely or never a careful ordering of influences for the promotion of clear intellectual activity. Such activity, when it exceeds that which is necessary to make the work of the teacher easy, is feared and repressed. This is natural enough, as long as women are excluded from the objects for which men are trained. While there are natural rights which women may not use, just claims which are not to be listened to, large objects which may not be approached, even in imagination, intellectual activity is dangerous: or, as the phrase is, unfit. Accordingly, marriage is the only object left open to woman. Philosophy she may pursue only fancifully, and under pain of ridicule: science only as a pastime, and under a similar penalty. Art is declared to be left open: but the necessary learning, and, yet more, the indispensable experience of reality, are denied to her. Literature is also said to be permitted: but under what penalties and restrictions? I need only refer to the last three pages of the review of Miss Sedgwick's last novel in the *North American Review,* to support all that can be said of the insolence to which the intellect of women is exposed in America. I am aware that many blush for that article, and disclaim all sympathy with it: but the bare fact that any man in the country could write it, that any editor could sanction it, that such an intolerable scoff should be allowed to find its way to the light, is a sufficient proof of the degradation of the sex. Nothing is thus left for women but marriage. —Yes; Religion, is the reply.—Religion is a temper, not a pursuit. It is the moral atmosphere in which human beings are to live and move. Men do not live to breathe: they breathe to live. A German lady of extraordinary powers and endowments, remarked to me with amazement on all the knowledge of the American women being based on theology. She observed that in her own country theology had its turn with other sciences, as a pursuit: but nowhere, but with the American women, had she known it make the foundation of all other knowledge. Even while thus complaining, this lady stated the case too favorably. American women have not the requisites for the study of theology. The difference between theology and religion, the science and the temper, is yet scarcely known among them. It is religion which they pursue as an occupation; and hence its small results upon the conduct, as well as upon the intellect. We are driven back upon marriage as the only appointed object in life: and upon the conviction that the sum and substance of female education in America, as in England, is training women to consider marriage as the sole object in life, and to pretend that they do not think so.

The morals of women are crushed. If there be any human power and business and privilege which is absolutely universal, it is the discovery and adoption of the principle and laws of duty. As every individual, whether man or woman, has a reason and a conscience, this is a work which each is thereby authorized to do for him or herself. But it is not only virtually prohibited to beings who, like the American women, have scarcely any objects in life proposed to them; but the whole apparatus of opinion is brought to bear offensively upon individuals among women who exercise freedom of mind in deciding upon what duty is, and the methods by which it is to be pursued. There is nothing extraordinary to the disinterested observer in women being so grieved at the case of slaves—slave wives and mothers, as well as spirit-broken men—as to wish to do what they could for their relief: there is nothing but what is natural in their being ashamed of the cowardice of such white slaves of the north as are deterred by intimidation from using their rights of speech and of the press, in behalf of the suffering race, and in their resolving not to do likewise: there is nothing but what is justifiable in their using their moral freedom, each for herself, in neglect of the threats of punishment: yet there were no bounds to the efforts made to crush the actions of women who thus used their human powers in the abolition question, and the convictions of those who looked on, and who might possibly be warmed into free action by the beauty of what they saw. It will be remembered that they were women who asserted the right of meeting and of discussion, on the day when Garrison was mobbed in Boston. Bills were posted about the city on this occasion, denouncing these women as casting off the refinement and delicacy of their sex: the newspapers, which laud the exertions of ladies in all other charities for the prosecution of which they are wont to meet and speak, teemed with the most disgusting reproaches and insinuations: and the pamphlets which related to the question all presumed to censure the act of duty which the women had performed in deciding upon their duty for themselves. . . .

How fearfully the morals of woman are crushed, appears from the prevalent persuasion that there are virtues which are peculiarly masculine, and others which are peculiarly feminine. It is amazing that a society which makes a most emphatic profession of its Christianity, should almost universally entertain such a fallacy: and not see that, in the case they suppose, instead of the character of Christ being the meeting point of all virtues, there would have been a separate gospel for women, and a second company of agents for its diffusion. It is not only that masculine and feminine employments are supposed to be properly different. No one in the world, I believe, questions this. But it is actually supposed that what are called the hardy virtues are more appropriate to men, and the gentler to women. As all virtues nourish each other, and can no otherwise be nourished, the consequence of the admitted fallacy is that men are, after all, not nearly so brave as they ought to be; nor women so gentle. But what is the manly character till it be gentle? The very word magnanimity cannot be thought of in relation to it till it becomes mild—Christ-like. Again, what can a woman be, or do, without bravery? Has she not to struggle with the toils and difficulties which follow upon the mere possession of a mind? Must she not face physical and moral pain—physical and moral danger? Is there a day of her life in which there are not conflicts wherein no one can help her—perilous work to be done, in which she can have neither sympathy nor aid? Let her lean upon man as much as he will, how much is it that he can do for her?—from how much can he protect her? From a few physical perils, and from a very few social evils. This is all. Over the moral world he has no control, except on his own account; and it is the moral life of human beings which is all in all. He can neither secure any woman from pain and grief, nor rescue her from the strife of emotions, nor prevent the film of life from cracking under her feet with every step she treads, nor hide from her the abyss which is beneath, nor save her from sinking into it at last alone. While it is so, while woman is human, men should beware how they deprive her of any of the strength which is all needed for the strife and burden of humanity. Let them beware how they put her off her watch and defense, by promises which they cannot fulfil;—promises of a guardianship which can arise only from within; of support which can be derived only from the freest moral action—from the self-reliance which can be generated by no other means.

But, it may be asked, how does society get on—what does it do? for it acts on the supposition of there being masculine and feminine virtues—upon the fallacy just exposed.

It does so; and the consequences are what might be looked for. Men are ungentle, tyrannical. They abuse the right of the strongest, however they may veil the abuse with indulgence. They want the magnanimity to discern woman's human rights; and they crush her morals rather than allow them. Women are, as might be anticipated, weak, ignorant and subservient, in as far as they exchange self-reliance for reliance on anything out of themselves. Those who will not submit to such a suspension of their moral functions (for the work of self-perfection remains to be done, sooner or later), have to suffer for their allegiance to duty. They have all the need of bravery that the few heroic men who assert the highest rights of women have of gentleness, to guard them from the encroachment to which power, custom, and education, incessantly conduce. . . .

Marriage

If there is any country on earth where the course of true love may be expected to run smooth, it is America. It is a country where all can marry early, where there need be no anxiety about a worldly provision, and where the troubles arising from conventional considerations of rank and connection ought to be entirely absent. It is difficult for a stranger to imagine beforehand why all should not love and marry naturally and freely, to the prevention of vice out of the marriage state, and of the common causes of unhapiness within it. The anticipations of the stranger are not, however, fulfilled: and they never can be while the one sex overbears the other. Marriage is in America more nearly universal, more safe, more tranquil, more fortunate than in England: but it is still subject to the troubles which arise from the inequality of the parties in mind and in occupation. It is more nearly universal, from the entire prosperity of the country: it is safer, from the greater freedom of divorce, and consequent discouragement of swindling, and other vicious marriages: it is more tranquil and fortunate from the marriage vows being made absolutely reciprocal; from the arrangements about property being generally far more favorable to the wife than in England; and from her not being made, as in England, to all intents and purposes the property of her husband. The outward requisites to happiness are nearly complete, and the institution is purified from the grossest of the scandals which degrade it in the Old World: but it is still the imperfect institution which it must remain while women continue to be ill-educated, passive, and subservient: or well-educated, vigorous, and free only upon sufferance. . . .

Occupation

The greater number of American women have home and its affairs, wherewith to occupy themselves. Wifely and motherly occupation may be called the sole business of woman there. If she has not that, she has nothing. The only alternative, as I have said, is making an occupation of either religion or dissipation; neither of which is fit to be so used: the one being a state of mind; the other altogether a negation when not taken in alternation with business.

It must happen that where all women have only one serious object, many of them will be unfit for that object. In the United States, as elsewhere, there are women no more fit to be wives and mothers than to be statesmen and generals. . . .

As for the occupations with which American ladies fill up their leisure; what has been already said will show that there is no great weight or diversity of occupation. Many are largely engaged in charities, doing good or harm according to the enlightenment of mind which is carried to the work. In New England, a vast deal of time is spent in attending preachings, and other religious meetings: and in paying visits, for religious purposes, to the poor and sorrowful. The same results follow from this practice that may be witnessed wherever it is much pursued. In as far as sympathy is kept up, and acquaintanceship between different classes in society is occasioned, the practice is good. In as far as it unsettles the minds of the visitors, encourages a false craving for religious excitement, tempts to spiritual interference on the one hand, and cant on the other, and humors or oppresses those who need such offices least, while it alienates those who want them most, the practice is bad. I am disposed to think that much good is done, and much harm: and that, whenever women have a greater charge of indispensable business on their hands, so as to do good and reciprocate religious sympathy by laying hold of opportunities, instead of by making occupation, more than the present good will be done, without any of the harm.

All American ladies are more or less literary: and some are so to excellent purpose: to the saving of their minds from vacuity. Readers are plentiful: thinkers are rare. Minds are of a very passive character: and it follows that languages are much cultivated. If ever a woman was pointed out to me as distinguished for information, I might be sure beforehand that she was a linguist. I met with a great number of ladies who read Latin; some Greek; some Hebrew; some German. With the exception of the last, the learning did not seem to be of much use to them, except as a harmless exercise. I met with more intellectual activity, more general power, among many ladies who gave little time to books, than among those who are distinguished as being literary. I did not meet with a good artist among all the ladies in the States. I never had the pleasure of seeing a good drawing, except in one instance; or, except in two, of hearing good music. The entire failure of all attempts to draw is still a mystery to me. The attempts are incessant; but the results are below criticism. Natural philosophy is not pursued to any extent by women. There is some pretension to mental and moral philosophy; but the less that is said on that head the better.

This is a sad account of things. It may tempt some to ask "what then are the American women?" They are better educated by Providence than by men. The lot of humanity is theirs: they have labor, probation, joy, and sorrow. They are good wives; and, under the teaching of nature, good mothers. They have, within the range of their activity, good sense, good temper, and good manners. Their beauty is very remarkable; and, I think, their wit no less. Their charity is overflowing, if it were but more enlightened: and it may be supposed that they could not exist without religion. It appears to superabound; but it is not usually of a healthy character. It may seem harsh to say this: but is it not the fact that religion emanates from the nature, from the moral state of the individual? Is it not therefore true that unless the nature be completely exercized, the moral state harmonized, the religion cannot be healthy?

One consequence, mournful and injurious, of the "chivalrous" taste and temper of a country with regard to its women is that it is difficult, where it is not impossible, for women to earn their bread. Where it as a boast that women do not labor, the encouragement and rewards of labor are not provided. It is so in America. In some parts, there are now so many women dependent on their own exertions for a maintenance, that the evil will give way before the force of circumstances. In the meantime, the lot of poor women is sad. Before the opening of the factories, there were but three resources: teaching, needlework, and keeping boardinghouses or hotels. Now, there are the mills; and women are employed in printing offices, as compositors, as well as folders and stitchers.

I dare not trust myself to do more than touch on this topic. There would be little use in dwelling upon it; for the mischief lies in the system by which women are depressed, so as to have the greater number of objects of pursuit placed beyond their reach, more than in any minor arrangements which might be rectified by an exposure of particular evils. I would only ask of philanthropists of all countries to inquire of physicians what is the state of health of [seamstresses]; and to judge thence whether it is not inconsistent with common humanity that women should depend for bread upon such employment. Let them inquire what is the recompense of this kind of labor, and then wonder if they can that the pleasures of the licentious are chiefly supplied from that class. Let them reverence the strength of such as keep their virtue, when the toil which they know is slowly and surely destroying them will barely afford them bread, while the wages of sin are luxury and idleness. During the present interval between the feudal age and the coming time, when life and its occupations will be freely thrown open to women as to men, the condition of the female working classes is such that if its sufferings were but made known, emotions of horror and shame would tremble through the whole of society.

For women who shrink from the lot of the needlewoman—almost equally dreadful, from the fashionable milliner down to the humble stocking-darner—for those who shrink through pride, or fear of sickness, poverty, or temptation, there is little resource but pretension to teach. . . . Ladies who fully deserve the confidence of society may realize an independence in a few years by school-keeping in the north: but, on the whole, the scanty reward of female labor in America remains the reproach to the country which its philanthropists have for some years proclaimed it to be. I hope they will persevere in their proclamation, though special methods of charity will not avail to cure the evil. It lies deep; it lies in the subordination of the sex: and upon this the exposures and remonstrances of philanthropists may ultimately succeed in fixing the attention of society; particularly of women. The progression or emancipation of any class usually, if not always, takes place through the efforts of individuals of that class: and so it must be here. All women should inform themselves of the condition of their sex, and of their own position. It must necessarily follow that the noblest of them will, sooner or later, put forth a moral power which shall prostrate cant, and burst asunder the bonds (silken to some, but cold iron to others) of feudal prejudices and usages. In the meantime, is it to be understood that the principles of the Declaration of Independence bear no relation to half of the human race? If so, what is the ground of the limitation? If not so, how is the restricted and dependent state of women to be reconciled with the proclamation that "all are endowed by their Creator with certain inalienable rights; that among these are life, liberty, and the pursuit of happiness?"

Catharine Beecher and Harriet Beecher Stowe
PRINCIPLES OF DOMESTIC SCIENCE (1870)

The authors of this volume, while they sympathize with every honest effort to relieve the disabilities and sufferings of their sex, are confident that the chief cause of these evils is the fact that the honor and duties of the family state are not duly appreciated, that women are not trained for these duties as men are trained for their trades and professions, and that, as the consequence, family labor is poorly done, poorly paid, and regarded as menial and disgraceful.

To be the nurse of young children, a cook, or a housemaid, is regarded as the lowest and last resort of poverty, and one which no woman of culture and position can assume without loss of caste and respectability.

It is the aim of this volume to elevate both the honor and the remuneration of all the employments that sustain the many difficult and sacred duties of the family state, and thus to render each department of woman's true profession as much desired and respected as are the most honored professions of men.

When the other sex are to be instructed in law, medicine, or divinity, they are favored with numerous institutions richly endowed, with teachers of the highest talents and acquirements, with extensive libraries, and abundant and costly apparatus. With such advantages they devote nearly ten of the best years of life to preparing themselves for their profession; and to secure the public from unqualified members of these professions, none can enter them until examined by a competent body, who certify to their due preparation for their duties.

From *Principles of Domestic Science . . . A Textbook* (New York, 1870).

Woman's profession embraces the care and nursing of the body in the critical periods of infancy and sickness, the training of the human mind in the most impressible period of childhood, the instruction and control of servants, and most of the government and economies of the family state. These duties of woman are as sacred and important as any ordained to man; and yet no such advantages for preparation have been accorded to her, nor is there any qualified body to certify the public that a woman is duly prepared to give proper instruction in her profession. . . .

During the upward progress of the age, and the advance of a more enlightened Christianity, the writers of this volume have gained more elevated views of the true mission of woman—of the dignity and importance of her distinctive duties, and of the true happiness which will be the reward of a right appreciation of this mission, and a proper performance of these duties.

There is at the present time an increasing agitation of the public mind, evolving many theories and some crude speculations as to woman's rights and duties. That there is a great social and moral power in her keeping, which is now seeking expression by organization, is manifest, and that resulting plans and efforts will involve some mistakes, some collisions, and some failures, all must expect.

But to intelligent, reflecting, and benevolent women—whose faith rests on the character and teachings of Jesus Christ—there are great principles revealed by him, which in the end will secure the grand result which he taught and suffered to achieve. It is hoped that in the following pages these principles will be so exhibited and illustrated as to aid in securing those rights and advantages which Christ's religion aims to provide for all, and especially for the most weak and defenseless of his children.

The Christian Family

. . . The distinctive feature of the family is self-sacrificing labor of the stronger and wiser members to raise the weaker and more ignorant to equal advantages. The father undergoes toil and self-denial to provide a home, and then the mother becomes a self-sacrificing laborer to train its inmates. . . .

The family state then, is the aptest earthly illustration of the heavenly kingdom, and in it woman is its chief minister. Her great

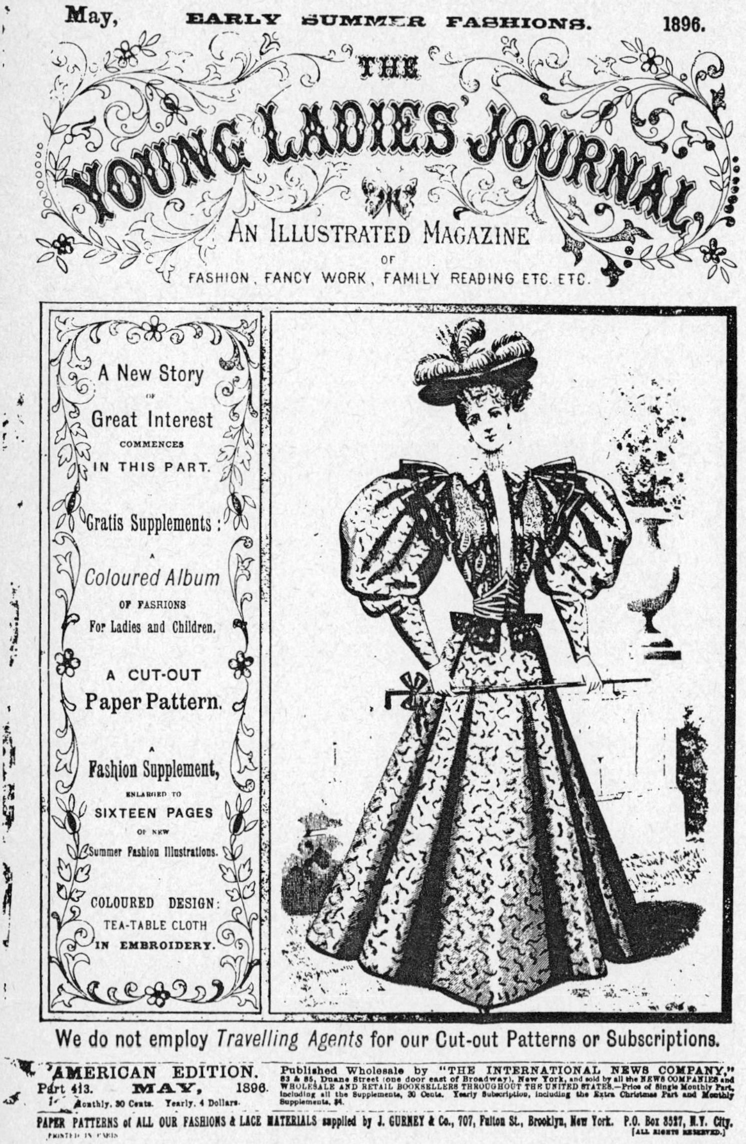
May, EARLY SUMMER FASHIONS. 1896.

THE YOUNG LADIES' JOURNAL

AN ILLUSTRATED MAGAZINE OF FASHION, FANCY WORK, FAMILY READING ETC. ETC.

A New Story of Great Interest COMMENCES IN THIS PART.

Gratis Supplements:

A *Coloured Album* OF FASHIONS For Ladies and Children.

A CUT-OUT Paper Pattern.

A Fashion Supplement, ENLARGED TO SIXTEEN PAGES OF NEW Summer Fashion Illustrations.

COLOURED DESIGN: TEA-TABLE CLOTH IN EMBROIDERY.

We do not employ *Travelling Agents* for our Cut-out Patterns or Subscriptions.

AMERICAN EDITION. Part 413. MAY, 1896. Monthly, 30 Cents. Yearly, 4 Dollars.

Published Wholesale by "THE INTERNATIONAL NEWS COMPANY," 83 & 85, Duane Street (one door east of Broadway), New York, and sold by all the NEWS COMPANIES and WHOLESALE AND RETAIL BOOKSELLERS THROUGHOUT THE UNITED STATES.—Price of Single Monthly Part, including all the Supplements, 30 Cents. Yearly Subscription, including the Extra Christmas Part and Monthly Supplements, $4.

PAPER PATTERNS of ALL OUR FASHIONS & LACE MATERIALS supplied by J. GURNEY & Co., 707, Fulton St., Brooklyn, New York. P.O. Box 3527, N.Y. City.

PRINTED IN PARIS [ALL RIGHTS RESERVED.]

FIGURE 3. The "feminine ideal" in nineteenth-century America was equated with submissiveness, proper attire, polite work, and the family.

mission is self-denial, in training its members to self-sacrificing labors for the ignorant and weak: if not her own children, then the neglected children of her Father in heaven. She is to rear all under her care to lay up treasures, not on earth, but in heaven. All the pleasures of this life end here; but those who train immortal minds are to reap the fruit of their labor through eternal ages.

To man is appointed the outdoor labor—to till the earth, dig the mines, toil in the foundries, traverse the ocean, transport merchandise, labor in manufactories, construct houses, conduct civil, municipal, and state affairs, and all the heavy work, which, most of the day, excludes him from the comforts of a home. But the great stimulus to all these toils, implanted in the heart of every true man, is the desire for a home of his own, and the hopes of paternity. Every man who truly lives for immortality responds to the beatitude, "Children are a heritage from the Lord: blessed is the man that hath his quiver full of them!" The more a father and mother live under the influence of that "immortality which Christ hath brought to light," the more is the blessedness of rearing a family understood and appreciated. Every child trained aright is to dwell forever in exalted bliss with those that gave it life and trained it for heaven.

The blessed privileges of the family state are not confined to those who rear children of their own. Any woman who can earn a livelihood, as every woman should be trained to do, can take a properly qualified female associate, and institute a family of her own, receiving to its heavenly influences the orphan, the sick, the homeless, and the sinful, and by motherly devotion train them to follow the self-denying example of Christ, in educating his earthly children for true happiness in this life and for his eternal home. . . .

. . . To the minds of most children and servants, "to be a lady," is almost synonymous with "to be waited on, and do no work." It is the earnest desire of the authors of this volume to make plain the falsity of this growing popular feeling, and to show how much happier and more efficient family life will become when it is strengthened, sustained, and adorned by family work.

Commentary

Gerda Lerner

THE LADY AND THE MILL GIRL: CHANGES IN THE STATUS OF WOMEN IN THE AGE OF JACKSON

According to Professor Gerda Lerner of Sarah Lawrence College, the American woman's status actually deteriorated, rather than improved, between the colonial period and the second half of the nineteenth century. Because of the shortage of women and the importance of their economic function in the English colonies, the colonial American woman's position was in some ways advantageous. Although theoretically her place in society was as a daughter or wife rather than as an individual, in practice allowances were made in her legal standing and there were opportunities to work outside of the home. Decisive changes occurred, Lerner contends, between 1800 and 1840 to alter this picture. Instead of inclusion in the egalitarian ideology that replaced the hierarchical concepts of colonial life, the woman's economic and social functions were narrowed, and she remained divorced from political power. At the same time that a man's position in society was increasingly dependent on ability (thus allowing for individual upward mobility and self-fulfillment), the woman was "by tacit consensus, excluded from the new democracy."

Further, Professor Lerner maintains that the industrial activity of the first half of the nineteenth century assisted this change in the status of woman by accenting and increasing the dissimilarities between women of different classes. Industrialization in effect opened up economic opportunities for the "mill girl," while it precluded work for the "lady." The latter's frustration was acute because she now faced an abundance of leisure with little meaningful work to do, especially as men professionalized her former vocations in the areas of medicine, practical law and the retail trades. In comparison, the mill girl's status, while high during the early development of the textile industry in New England, had waned by the late 1830s as immigrants replaced native-born farm girls. As distinctions between the work of men and women in factories were sharpened, women were given the lowest-paid, least-skilled jobs. Yet in some ways the status of the lady and mill girl was similar. Both were isolated from decision-making and were acted upon by a male-oriented society beyond their control.

Reprinted by permission from *American Studies Journal* (Spring, 1969), pp. 5–15. Footnotes omitted.

The period 1800–1840 is one in which decisive changes occurred in the status of American women. It has remained surprisingly unexplored. With the exception of a recent, unpublished dissertation by Keith Melder and the distinctive work of Elisabeth Dexter, there is a dearth of descriptive material and an almost total absence of interpretation. Yet the period offers essential clues to an understanding of later institutional developments, particularly the shape and nature of the women's rights movement. This analysis will consider the economic, political and social status of women and examine the changes in each area. It will also attempt an interpretation of the ideological shifts which occurred in American society concerning the "proper" role for women.

Periodization always offers difficulties. It seemed useful here, for purposes of comparison, to group women's status before 1800 roughly under the "colonial" heading and ignore the transitional and possibly atypical shifts which occurred during the American Revolution and the early period of nationhood. Also, regional differences were largely ignored. The South was left out of consideration entirely because its industrial development occurred later.

The status of colonial women has been well studied and described and can briefly be summarized for comparison with the later period. Throughout the colonial period there was a marked shortage of women, which varied with the regions and always was greatest in the frontier areas. This (from the point of view of women) favorable sex ratio enhanced their status and position. The Puritan world view regarded idleness as sin; life in an underdeveloped country made it absolutely necessary that each member of the community perform an economic function. Thus work for women, married or single, was not only approved, it was regarded as a civic duty. Puritan town councils expected single girls, widows and unattached women to be self-supporting and for a long time provided needy spinsters with parcels of land. There was no social sanction against married women working; on the contrary, wives were expected to help their husbands in their trade and won social approval for doing extra work in or out of the home. Needy children, girls as well as boys, were indentured or apprenticed and were expected to work for their keep.

The vast majority of women worked within their homes, where their labor produced most articles needed for the family. The entire colonial production of cloth and clothing and partially that of shoes was in the hands of women. In addition to these occupations, women were found in many different kinds of employment. They were butchers, silversmiths, gunsmiths, upholsterers. They ran mills, plantations, tan yards, shipyards and every kind of shop, tavern and boarding house. They were gate keepers, jail keepers, sextons, journalists, printers, "doctoresses," apothecaries, midwives, nurses and teachers. Women acquired their skills the same way as did the men, through apprenticeship training, frequently within their own families.

Absence of a dowry, ease of marriage and remarriage and a more lenient attitude of the law with regard to woman's property rights were manifestations of the improved position of wives in the colonies. Under British common law, marriage destroyed a woman's contractual capacity; she could not sign a contract even with the consent of her husband. But colonial authorities were more lenient toward the wife's property rights by protecting her dower rights in her husband's property, granting her personal clothing and upholding prenuptial contracts between husband and wife. In the absence of the husband, colonial courts granted women "femme sole" rights, which enabled them to conduct their husband's business, sign contracts and sue. The relative social freedom of women and the esteem in which they were held was commented upon by most early foreign travelers in America.

But economic, legal and social status tell only part of the story. Colonial society as a whole was hierarchical, and rank and standing in society depended on the position of the men. Women did not play a determining role in the ranking pattern; they took their position in society through the men of their own family or the men they married. In other words, they participated in the hierarchy only as daughters and wives, not as individuals. Similarly, their occupations were, by and large, merely auxiliary, designed to contribute to family income, enhance their husbands' business or continue it in case of widowhood. The self-supporting spinsters were certainly the exception. The underlying assumption of colonial society was that women ought to occupy an inferior and subordinate position. The settlers had brought this assumption with them from Europe; it was reflected in their legal concepts, their willingness to exclude women from political life, their discriminatory educational practices. What is remarkable is the extent to which this felt inferiority of women was constantly challenged and modified under the impact of environment, frontier conditions and a favorable sex ratio.

By 1840 all of American society had changed. The Revolution had substituted an egalitarian ideology for the hierarchical concepts of colonial life. Privilege based on ability rather than inherited status, upward mobility for all groups of society and unlimited opportunities for individual self-fulfillment had become ideological goals, if not always realities. For men, that is; women were, by tacit consensus, excluded from the new democracy. Indeed their actual situation had in many respects deteriorated. While, as wives, they had benefitted from increasing wealth, urbanization, and industrialization, their role as economic producers and as political members of society differed sharply from that of men. Women's work outside of the home no longer met with social approval; on the contrary, with two notable exceptions, it was condemned. Many business and professional occupations formerly open to women were now closed, many others restricted as to training and advancement. The entry of large numbers of women into low status, low pay and low skill industrial work had fixed such work by definition as "woman's work." Women's political status, while legally unchanged, had deteriorated relative to the advances made by men. At the same time the genteel lady of fashion had become a model of American femininity and the definition of "woman's proper sphere" seemed narrower and more confined than ever.

Within the scope of this article only a few of these changes can be more fully explained. The professionalization of medicine and its impact on women may serve as a typical example of what occurred in all the professions.

In colonial America there were no medical schools, no medical journals, few hospitals and few laws pertaining to the practice of the healing arts. Clergymen and governors, barbers, quacks, apprentices and women practiced medicine. Most practitioners acquired their credentials by reading Paracelsus and Galen and serving an apprenticeship with an established practitioner. Among the semi-trained "physics," surgeons and healers the occasional "doctoress" was fully accepted and frequently well rewarded. County records of all the colonies contain references to the work of the female physicians. There was even a female army surgeon, a Mrs. Allyn, who served during King Philip's war. Plantation records mention by name several slave women who were granted special privileges because of their useful service as midwives and "doctoresses."

The period of the professionalization of American medicine dates from 1765, when Dr. William Shippen began his lectures on mid-wifery in Philadelphia. The founding of medical faculties in several colleges, the standardization of training requirements and the prolif-eration of medical societies intensified during the last quarter of the eighteenth century. The American Revolution dramatized the need for trained medical personnel, afforded firsthand battlefield experi-ence to a number of surgeons and brought increasing numbers of semi-trained practitioners in contact with the handful of European-trained surgeons working in the military hospitals. This was an experience from which women were excluded. The resulting interest in improved medical training, the gradual appearance of graduates of medical colleges and the efforts of medical societies led to licens-ing legislation. In 1801 Maryland required all medical practitioners to be licensed; in 1806 New York enacted a similar law, providing for an examination before a commission. By the late 1820s all states except three had set up licensing requirements. Since most of these laws stipulated attendance at a medical college as one of the pre-requisites for licensing, women were automatically excluded. By the 1830s the few established female practitioners who might have continued their practice in the old ways had probably died out. Whatever vested interest they had had was too weak to assert itself against the new profession. . . .

In the field of midwifery the results were similar, but the process was more complicated. Women had held a virtual monopoly in the profession in colonial America. In 1646 a man was prosecuted in Maine for practicing as a midwife. There are many records of well-trained midwives with diplomas from European institutions working in the colonies. In most of the colonies midwives were licensed, registered and required to pass an examination before a board. When Dr. Shippen announced his pioneering lectures on midwifery, he did it to "combat the widespread popular prejudice against the man-midwife" and because he considered most midwives ignorant and improperly trained.

Yet he invited "those women who love virtue enough, to own their Ignorance, and apply for instruction" to attend his lectures, offering as an inducement the assurance that female pupils would be taught privately. It is not known if any midwives availed themselves of the opportunity.

Technological advances, as well as scientific, worked against the interests of female midwives. In sixteenth-century Europe the invention and use of the obstetrical forceps had for three generations been the well-kept secret of the Chamberlen family and had greatly enhanced their medical practice. Hugh Chamberlen was forced by circumstances to sell the secret to the Medical College in Amsterdam, which in turn transmitted the precious knowledge to licensed physicians only. By the time the use of the instrument became widespread it had become associated with male physicians and midwives. Similarly in America, introduction of the obstetrical forceps was associated with the practice of male midwives and served to their advantage. By the end of the eighteenth century a number of male physicians advertised their practice of midwifery. Shortly thereafter female midwives also resorted to advertising, probably in an effort to meet the competition. By the early nineteenth century male physicians had virtually monopolized the practice of midwifery on the eastern seaboard. True to the generally delayed economic development in the western frontier regions, female midwives continued to work on the frontier until a much later period. It is interesting to note that the concepts of "propriety" shifted with the prevalent practice. In seventeenth-century Maine the attempt of a man to act as a midwife was considered outrageous and illegal; in mid-nineteenth-century America the suggestion that women should train as midwives and physicians was considered equally outrageous and improper.

Professionalization, similar to that in medicine with the elimination of women from the upgraded profession, occurred in the field of law. Before 1750, when law suits were commonly brought to the courts by the plaintiffs themselves or by deputies without specialized legal training, women as well as men could and did act as "attorneys-in-fact." When the law became a paid profession and trained lawyers took over litigation, women disappeared from the court scene for over a century.

A similar process of shrinking opportunities for women developed in business and in the retail trades. There were fewer female storekeepers and business women in the 1830s than there had been in colonial days. There was also a noticeable shift in the kind of merchandise handled by them. Where previously women could be found running almost every kind of retail shop, after 1830 they were mostly found in businesses which served women only.

The only fields in which professionalization did not result in the elimination of women from the upgraded profession were nursing and teaching. Both were characterized by a severe shortage of labor. Nursing lies outside the field of this inquiry since it did not become an organized profession until after the Civil War. Before then it was regarded peculiarly as a woman's occupation, although some of the hospitals and the army during wars employed male nurses. These bore the stigma of low skill, low status and low pay. Generally, nursing was regarded as simply an extension of the unpaid services performed by the housewife—a characteristic attitude that haunts the profession to this day.

Education seems, at first glance, to offer an entirely opposite pattern from that of the other professions. In colonial days women had taught "dame schools" and grade schools during summer sessions. Gradually, as educational opportunities for girls expanded, they advanced just a step ahead of their students. Professionalization of teaching occurred between 1820–1860, a period marked by a sharp increase in the number of women teachers. The spread of female seminaries, academies and normal schools provided new opportunities for the training and employment of female teachers.

This trend which runs counter to that found in the other professions can be accounted for by the fact that women filled a desperate need created by the challenge of the common schools, the ever-increasing size of the student body and the westward growth of the nation. America was committed to educating its children in public schools, but it was insistent on doing so as cheaply as possible. Women were available in great numbers and they were willing to work cheaply. The result was another ideological adaptation: in the very period when the gospel of the home as woman's only proper sphere was preached most loudly, it was discovered that women were the natural teachers of youth, could do the job better than men and were to be preferred for such employment. This was always provided, of course, that they would work at the proper wage differential—30–50 percent of the wages paid male teachers was considered appropriate. . . .

There was another field in which the labor of women was appreciated and which they were urged to enter—industry. . . .

American industrialization, which occurred in an underdeveloped economy with a shortage of labor, depended on the labor of women and children. Men were occupied with agricultural work and were not available or willing to enter the factories. This accounts for the special features of the early development of the New England textile industry: the relatively high wages, the respectability of the job and relatively high status of the mill girls, the patriarchal character of the model factory towns and the temporary mobility of women workers from farm to factory and back again to farm. All this was characteristic only of a limited area and of a period of about two decades. By the late 1830s the romance had worn off; immigration had supplied a strongly competitive, permanent work force willing to work for subsistence wages; early efforts at trade union organization had been shattered and mechanization had turned semiskilled factory labor into unskilled labor. The process led to the replacement of the New England-born farm girls by immigrants in the mills and was accompanied by a loss of status and respectability for female workers.

The lack of organized social services during periods of depression drove ever greater numbers of women into the labor market. At first, inside the factories distinctions between men's and women's jobs were blurred. Men and women were assigned to machinery on the basis of local need. But as more women entered industry the limited number of occupations open to them tended to increase competition among them, thus lowering pay standards. Generally, women regarded their work as temporary and hesitated to invest in apprenticeship training, because they expected to marry and raise families. Thus they remained untrained, casual labor and were soon, by custom, relegated to the lowest paid, least skilled jobs. Long hours, overwork and poor working conditions would characterize women's work in industry for almost a century.

Another result of industrialization was in increasing differences in life styles between women of different classes. When female occupations, such as carding, spinning and weaving, were transferred from home to factory, the poorer women followed their traditional work and became industrial workers. The women of the middle and upper classes could use their newly gained time for leisure pursuits: they became ladies. And a small but significant group among

FIGURE 4. The "factory girl's" status was usually low and her working conditions sub-standard. *(State Historical Society of Wisconsin)*

them chose to prepare themselves for professional careers by advanced education. This group would prove to be the most vocal and troublesome in the near future.

As class distinctions sharpened, social attitudes toward women became polarized. The image of "the lady" was elevated to the accepted ideal of femininity toward which all women would strive. In this formulation of values lower-class women were simply ignored. The actual lady was, of course, nothing new on the American scene; she had been present ever since colonial days. What was new in the 1830s was the cult of the lady, her elevation to a status symbol. The advancing prosperity of the early nineteenth century made it possible for middle-class women to aspire to the status formerly reserved for upper-class women. The "cult of true womanhood" of the 1830s became a vehicle for such aspirations. Mass circulation newspapers and magazines made it possible to teach every woman how to elevate the status of her family by setting "proper" standards of behavior, dress and literary tastes. *Godey's Lady's Book* and innumerable gift books and tracts of the period all preach the same gospel of "true womanhood"—piety, purity, domesticity. Those unable to reach the goal of becoming ladies were to be satisfied with the lesser goal—acceptance of their "proper place" in the home.

It is no accident that the slogan "woman's place is in the home" took on a certain aggressiveness and shrillness precisely at the time when increasing numbers of poorer women *left* their homes to become factory workers. Working women were not a fit subject for the concern of publishers and mass-media writers. Idleness, once a disgrace in the eyes of society, had become a status symbol. Thorstein Veblen, one of the earliest and sharpest commentators on the subject, observed that it had become almost the sole social function of the lady "to put in evidence her economic unit's ability to pay." She was "a means of conspicuously unproductive expenditure," devoted to displaying her husband's wealth. Just as the cult of white womanhood in the South served to preserve a labor and social system based on race distinctions, so did the cult of the lady in an egalitarian society serve as a means of preserving class distinctions. Where class distinctions were not so great, as on the frontier, the position of women was closer to what it had been in colonial days; their economic contribution was more highly valued, their opportunities were less restricted and their positive participation in community life was taken for granted.

In the urbanized and industrialized Northeast the life experience of middle-class women was different in almost every respect from that of the lower-class women. But there was one thing the society lady and the mill girl had in common—they were equally disfranchised and isolated from the vital centers of power. Yet the political status of women had not actually deteriorated. With very few exceptions women had neither voted nor stood for office during the colonial period. Yet the spread of the franchise to ever wider groups of white males during the Jacksonian age, the removal of property restrictions, the increasing number of immigrants who acquired access to the franchise, made the gap between these new enfranchised voters and the disfranchised women more obvious. Quite naturally, educated and propertied women felt this deprivation more keenly. Their own career expectations had been encouraged by widening educational opportunities; their consciousness of their own abilities and of their potential for power had been enhanced by their activities in the reform movements of the 1830s; the general spirit of upward mobility and venturesome entrepreneurship that pervaded the Jacksonian era was infectious. But in the late 1840s a sense of acute frustration enveloped these educated and highly spirited women. Their rising expectations had met with frustration, their hopes had been shattered; they were bitterly conscious of a relative lowering of status and a loss of position. This sense of frustration led them to action; it was one of the main factors in the rise of the woman's rights movement.

The women, who in 1848 declared boldly and with considerable exaggeration that "the history of mankind is a history of repeated injuries and usurpations on the part of man toward woman, having in direct object the establishment of an absolute tyranny over her," did not speak for the truly exploited and abused working woman. As a matter of fact, they were largely ignorant of her condition and, with the notable exception of Susan B. Anthony, indifferent to her fate. But they judged from the realities of their own life experience. Like most revolutionaries, they were not the most downtrodden but rather the most status-deprived group. Their frustrations and traditional isolation from political power funneled their discontent into fairly utopian declarations and immature organizational means. They would learn better in the long, hard decades of practical struggle. Yet it is their initial emphasis on the legal and political "disabilities" of women which has provided the framework for most of the historical work on women. For almost a hundred years sympathetic historians have told the story of women in America from the feminist viewpoint. Their tendency has been to reason from the position of middle-class women to a generalization concerning all American women. This distortion has obscured the actual and continuous contributions of women to American life. To avoid such a distortion, any valid generalization concerning American women after the 1830s should reflect a recognition of class stratification.

For lower-class women the changes brought by industrialization were actually advantageous, offering income and advancement opportunities, however limited, and a chance for participation in the ranks of organized labor. They, by and large, tended to join men in their struggle for economic advancement and became increasingly concerned with economic gains and protective labor legislation. Middle- and upper-class women, on the other hand, reacted to actual and fancied status deprivation by increasing militancy and the formation of organizations for women's rights, by which they meant especially legal and property rights.

The four decades preceding the Seneca Falls Convention were decisive in the history of American women. They brought an actual deterioration in the economic opportunities open to women, a relative deterioration in their political status and a rising level of expectation and subsequent frustration in a privileged elite group of educated women. The ideology still pervasive in our present-day society regarding woman's "proper" role was formed in those decades. Later, under the impact of feminist attacks this ideology would grow defensive and attempt to bolster its claims by appeals to universality and pretentions to a history dating back to antiquity or, at least, to the *Mayflower.* Women, we are told, have always played a restricted and subordinate role in American life. In fact, however, it was in mid-nineteenth-century America that the ideology of "woman's place is in the home" changed from being an accurate description of existing reality into a myth. It became the "feminine mystique"—a longing for a lost, archaic world of agrarian family self-sufficiency, updated by woman's consumer function and the misunderstood dicta of Freudian psychology.

The decades 1800–1840 also provide the clues to an understanding of the institutional shape of the later women's organizations. These would be led by middle-class women whose self-image, life experience and ideology had largely been fashioned and influenced by these early, transitional years. The concerns of middle-class women—property rights, the franchise and moral uplift—would dominate the women's rights movement. But side by side with it, and at times cooperating with it, would grow a number of organizations serving the needs of working women.

American women were the largest disfranchised group in the nation's history, and they retained this position longer than any other group. Although they found ways of making their influence felt continuously, not only as individuals but as organized groups, power eluded them. The mill girl and the lady, both born in the age of Jackson, would not gain access to power until they learned to cooperate, each for her own separate interests. It would take almost six decades before they would find common ground. The issue around which they finally would unite and push their movement to victory was the "impractical and utopian" demand raised at Seneca Falls—the means to power in American society—female suffrage.

Further Reading

The more general sources for studying the colonial woman are summarized in the "Suggestions for Additional Reading" at the end of this book. In addition to these readings, Professor Lerner employed the following secondary material: K. C. Hurd-Mead, *A History of Women in Medicine: From the Earliest Times to the Beginning of the 19th Century* (Haddam, Conn., 1938); Sophie H. Drinker, "Women Attorneys of Colonial Times," *Maryland Historical Society Bulletin* (December 1961); Edith Abbott, *Women in Industry* (New York, 1910); Helen L. Summer, *History of Women in Industry in the United States,* in *Report on Conditions of Woman and Child Wage-Earners in the United States,* 19 vols. (Washington, D.C., 1910) Vol. 9; and Elizabeth F. Baker, *Technology and Woman's Work* (New York, 1964), Chapters 1–5. Also consult Mathew Carey, *Miscellaneous Essays* (Phila., 1830), pp. 153–203; and Thorstein Veblen, "The Economic Theory of Woman's Dress," *Essays in Our Changing Order,* edited by Leon Ardzrooni (New York, 1934), pp. 65–77.

Barbara Welter

THE CULT OF TRUE WOMANHOOD, 1820-1860

In the following article, Barbara Welter, a member of the history department at Hunter College, City University of New York, takes a scrupulous look at the ideology supportive of the "lady" between 1820 and 1860. Focusing upon the portrait of the American woman present in women's magazines, gift annuals, and religious literature, Professor Welter finds that women were encouraged to define themselves exclusively in terms of the home. The advocates of the cult of "True Womanhood," interestingly, were not limited to male counselors. From the pens of domestic reformers such as Catharine Beecher, Lydia Maria Child, Sarah Josepha Hale and Lydia Sigourney came admonitions that middle- and upper-class women should fulfill their "feminine nature" by embracing without reservations the four virtues of "piety, purity, submissiveness and domesticity." Welter notes that as nineteenth-century American men became less concerned about creating a righteous society and more occupied with obtaining material possessions, they promoted an ideology that obligated women to be a personification of goodness. Likewise, the greater freedom men had acquired to be involved in public life, the more they insisted that women remain in the home. In a world increasingly perplexing and uncertain, womanhood was portrayed in absolute terms; the less men were willing to admit their own emotions, the more women were singled out as "heart." This normative understanding of femininity further affirmed that women should be restricted to the domestic circle for their own good. Otherwise, their delicate natures would be scarred by the harsh and debilitating influences of public life. In the America de Tocqueville found "more democratic," the domestic sphere was becoming a cloister for women.

The nineteenth-century American man was a busy builder of bridges and railroads, at work long hours in a materialistic society. The religious values of his forebears were neglected in practice if not in intent, and he occasionally felt some guilt that he had turned this new land, this temple of the chosen people, into one vast counting-house. But he could salve his conscience by reflecting that he had left behind a hostage, not only to fortune, but to all the values which he held so dear and treated so lightly. Woman, in the cult of True Womanhood presented by the women's magazines, gift annuals and

Reprinted by permission from the *American Quarterly* (Summer, 1966, Part I), pp. 151–74. Copyright © 1966, Trustees of the University of Pennsylvania. Footnotes omitted.

religious literature of the nineteenth century, was the hostage in the home. In a society where values changed frequently, where fortunes rose and fell with frightening rapidity, where social and economic mobility provided instability as well as hope, one thing at least remained the same—a true woman was a true woman, wherever she was found. If anyone, male or female, dared to tamper with the complex of virtues which made up True Womanhood, he was damned immediately as an enemy of God, of civilization and of the Republic. It was a fearful obligation, a solemn responsibility, which the nineteenth-century American woman had—to uphold the pillars of the temple with her frail white hand.

The attributes of True Womanhood, by which a woman judged herself and was judged by her husband, her neighbors and society could be divided into four cardinal virtues—piety, purity, submissiveness and domesticity. Put them all together and they spelled mother, daughter, sister, wife—woman. Without them, no matter whether there was fame, achievement or wealth, all was ashes. With them she was promised happiness and power.

Religion or piety was the core of woman's virtue, the source of her strength. Young men looking for a mate were cautioned to search first for piety, for if that were there, all else would follow. Religion belonged to woman by divine right, a gift of God and nature. This "peculiar susceptibility" to religion was given her for a reason: "the vestal flame of piety, lighted up by Heaven in the breast of woman" would throw its beams into the naughty world of men. So far would its candlepower reach that the "Universe might be Enlightened, Improved, and Harmonized by *woman!!*" She would be another, better Eve, working in cooperation with the Redeemer, bringing the world back "from its revolt and sin." The world would be reclaimed for God through her suffering, for "God increased the cares and sorrows of woman, that she might be sooner constrained to accept the terms of salvation." A popular poem by Mrs. Frances Osgood, "The Triumph of the Spiritual Over the Sensual" expressed just this sentiment, woman's purifying passionless love bringing an erring man back to Christ.

Dr. Charles Meigs, explaining to a graduating class of medical students why women were naturally religious, said that "hers is a pious mind. Her confiding nature leads her more readily than men to accept the proffered grace of the Gospel." Caleb Atwater, Esq., writing in *The Ladies' Repository,* saw the hand of the Lord in female piety: "Religion is exactly what a woman needs, for it gives her that dignity that best suits her dependence." And Mrs. John Sandford, who had no very high opinion of her sex, agreed thoroughly: "Religion is just what woman needs. Without it she is ever restless or unhappy. . . ." Mrs. Sandford and the others did not speak only of that restlessness of the human heart, which St. Augustine notes, that can only find its peace in God. They spoke rather of religion as a kind of tranquilizer for the many undefined longings which swept even the most pious young girl, and about which it was better to pray than to think.

One reason religion was valued was that it did not take a woman away from her "proper sphere," her home. Unlike participation in other societies or movements, church work would not make her less domestic or submissive, less a True Woman. In religious vineyards, said the *Young Ladies' Literary and Missionary Report,* "you may labor without the apprehension of detracting from the charms of feminine delicacy." Mrs. S. L. Dagg, writing from her chapter of the Society in Tuscaloosa, Alabama, was equally reassuring: "As no sensible woman will suffer her intellectual pursuits to clash with her domestic duties" she should concentrate on religious work "which promotes these very duties."

The women's seminaries aimed at aiding women to be religious, as well as accomplished. Mt. Holyoke's catalogue promised to make female education "a handmaid to the Gospel and an efficient auxiliary in the great task of renovating the world." The Young Ladies' Seminary at Bordentown, New Jersey, declared its most important function to be "the forming of a sound and virtuous character." In Keene, New Hampshire, the Seminary tried to instill a "consistent and useful character" in its students, to enable them in this life to be "a good friend, wife and mother" but more important, to qualify them for "the enjoyment of Celestial Happiness in the life to come." And Joseph M' D. Mathews, principal of Oakland Female Seminary in Hillsborough, Ohio, believed that "female education should be preeminently religious."

If religion was so vital to a woman, irreligion was almost too awful to contemplate. Women were warned not to let their literary or intellectual pursuits take them away from God. Sarah Josepha Hale spoke darkly of those who, like Margaret Fuller, threw away the "One True Book" for others, open to error. Mrs. Hale used the unfortunate Miss Fuller as fateful proof that "the greater the intellectual force, the greater and more fatal the errors into which women fall who wander from the Rock of Salvation, Christ the Saviour. . . ."

One gentleman, writing on "Female Irreligion" reminded his readers that "Man may make himself a brute, and does so very often, but can woman brutify herself to his level—the lowest level of human nature—without exerting special wonder?" Fanny Wright, because she was godless, "was no woman, mother though she be." A few years ago, he recalls, such women would have been whipped. In any case, "woman never looks lovelier than in her reverence for religion" and, conversely, "female irreligion is the most revolting feature in human character."

Purity was as essential as piety to a young woman, its absence as unnatural and unfeminine. Without it she was, in fact, no woman at all, but a member of some lower order. A "fallen woman" was a "fallen angel," unworthy of the celestial company of her sex. To contemplate the loss of purity brought tears; to be guilty of such a crime, in the women's magazines at least, brought madness or death. Even the language of the flowers had bitter words for it: a dried white rose symbolized "Death Preferable to Loss of Innocence." The marriage night was the single great event of a woman's life, when she bestowed her greatest treasure upon her husband, and from that time on was completely dependent upon him, an empty vessel, without legal or emotional existence of her own.

Therefore all True Women were urged, in the strongest possible terms, to maintain their virtue, although men, being by nature more sensual than they, would try to assault it. Thomas Branagan admitted in *The Excellency of the Female Character Vindicated* that his sex would sin and sin again, they could not help it, but woman, stronger and purer, must not give in and let man "take liberties incompatible with her delicacy." "If you do," Branagan addressed his gentle reader, "you will be left in silent sadness to bewail your credulity, imbecility, duplicity, and premature prostitution."

Mrs. Eliza Farrar, in *The Young Lady's Friend,* gave practical logistics to avoid trouble: "Sit not with another in a place that is too narrow; read not out of the same book; let not your eagerness to see anything induce you to place your head close to another person's."

If such good advice was ignored the consequences were terrible and inexorable. In *Girlhood and Womanhood: Or Sketches of My Schoolmates,* by Mrs. A. J. Graves (a kind of mid-nineteenth-century *The Group*), the bad ends of a boarding school class of girls are scrupulously recorded. The worst end of all is reserved for "Amelia Dorrington: The Lost One." Amelia died in the almshouse "the wretched victim of depravity and intemperance" and all because her mother had let her be "high-spirited not prudent." These girlish high spirits had been misinterpreted by a young man, with disastrous results. Amelia's "thoughtless levity" was "followed by a total loss of virtuous principle" and Mrs. Graves editorializes that "the coldest reserve is more admirable in a woman a man wishes to make his wife, than the least approach to undue familiarity." . . .

If, however, a woman managed to withstand man's assaults on her virtue, she demonstrated her superiority and her power over him. Eliza Farnham, trying to prove this female superiority, concluded smugly that "the purity of women is the everlasting barrier against which the tides of man's sensual nature surge." . . .

Men could be counted on to be grateful when women thus saved them from themselves. William Alcott, guiding young men in their relations with the opposite sex, told them that "Nothing is better calculated to preserve a young man from contamination of low pleasures and pursuits than frequent intercourse with the more refined and virtuous of the other sex." And he added, one assumes in equal innocence, that youths should "observe and learn to admire, that purity and ignorance of evil which is the characteristic of well-educated young ladies, and which, when we are near them, raises us above those sordid and sensual considerations which hold such sway over men in their intercourse with each other." . . .

Sometimes, however, a woman did not see the dangers to her treasure. In that case, they must be pointed out to her, usually by a male. In the nineteenth century any form of social change was tantamount to an attack on woman's virtue, if only it was correctly understood. For example, dress reform seemed innocuous enough and the bloomers worn by the lady of that name and her followers were certainly modest attire. Such was the reasoning only of the ignorant. In another issue of *The Ladies' Wreath* a young lady is represented in dialogue with her "Professor." The girl expresses admiration for the bloomer costume—it gives freedom of motion, is healthful and attractive. The "Professor" sets her straight. Trousers, he explains, are "only one of the many manifestations of that wild spirit of socialism and agrarian radicalism which is at present so rife in our land." The young lady recants immediately: "If this dress has any connexion with Fourierism or Socialism, or fanaticism in any shape whatever, I have no disposition to wear it at all . . . no true woman would so far compromise her delicacy as to espouse, however unwittingly, such a cause." . . .

Submission was perhaps the most feminine virtue expected of women. Men were supposed to be religious, although they rarely had time for it, and supposed to be pure, although it came awfully hard to them, but men were the movers, the doers, the actors. Women were the passive, submissive responders. The order of dialogue was, of course, fixed in Heaven. Man was "woman's superior by God's appointment, if not in intellectual dowry, at least by official decree." Therefore, as Charles Elliott argued in *The Ladies' Repository,* she should submit to him "for the sake of good order at least." In *The Ladies Companion* a young wife was quoted approvingly as saying that she did not think woman should "feel and act for herself" because "When, next to God, her husband is not the tribunal to which her heart and intellect appeals—the golden bowl of affection is broken." Women were warned that if they tampered with this quality they tampered with the order of the universe. . . .

Mrs. Sigourney, however, assured young ladies that although they were separate, they were equal. This difference of the sexes did not imply inferiority, for it was part of that same order of Nature established by Him "who bids the oak brave the fury of the tempest, and the alpine flower lean its cheek on the bosom of eternal snows." Dr. Meigs had a different analogy to make the same point, contrasting the anatomy of the Apollo of the Belvedere (illustrating the male principle) with the Venus de Medici (illustrating the female principle). "Woman," said the physician, with a kind of clinical gallantry, "has a head almost too small for intellect but just big enough for love." . . .

Woman then, in all her roles, accepted submission as her lot. It was a lot she had not chosen or deserved. As *Godey's* said, "the lesson of submission is forced upon woman." Without comment or criticism the writer affirms that "To suffer and to be silent under suffering seems the great command she has to obey." George Burnap referred to a woman's life as "a series of suppressed emotions."

She was, as Emerson said, "more vulnerable, more infirm, more mortal than man." The death of a beautiful woman, cherished in fiction, represented woman as the innocent victim, suffering without sin, too pure and good for this world but too weak and passive to resist its evil forces. The best refuge for such a delicate creature was the warmth and safety of her home.

The true woman's place was unquestionably by her own fireside —as daughter, sister, but most of all as wife and mother. Therefore domesticity was among the virtues most prized by the women's magazines. "As society is constituted," wrote Mrs. S. E. Farley, on the "Domestic and Social Claims on Woman," "the true dignity and beauty of the female character seem to consist in a right understanding and faithful and cheerful performance of social and family duties." Sacred Scripture reenforced social pressure: "St. Paul knew what was best for women when he advised them to be domestic," said Mrs. Sandford. "There is composure at home; there is something sedative in the duties which home involves. It affords security not only from the world, but from delusions and errors of every kind." . . .

One of the most important functions of woman as comforter was her role as nurse. Her own health was probably, although regettably, delicate. Many homes had "little sufferers," those pale children who wasted away to saintly deaths. And there were enough other illnesses of youth and age, major and minor, to give the nineteenth-century American woman nursing experience. The sickroom called for the exercise of her higher qualities of patience, mercy and gentleness as well as for her housewifely arts. She could thus fulfill her dual feminine function—beauty and usefulness. . . .

Nursing the sick, particularly sick males, not only made a woman feel useful and accomplished, but increased her influence. In a piece of heavy-handed humor in *Godey's* a man confessed that some women were only happy when their husbands were ailing that they might have the joy of nursing him to recovery "thus gratifying their medical vanity and their love of power by making him more dependent upon them." In a similar vein a husband sometimes suspected his wife "almost wishes me dead—for the pleasure of being utterly inconsolable."

In the home women were not only the highest adornment of civilization, but they were supposed to keep busy at morally uplifting tasks. Fortunately most of housework, if looked at in true womanly fashion, could be regarded as uplifting. Mrs. Sigourney extolled its virtues: "The science of housekeeping affords exercise for the judgment and energy, ready recollection, and patient self-possession, that are the characteristics of a superior mind." According to Mrs. Farrar, making beds was good exercise, the repetitiveness of routine tasks inculcated patience and perseverance, and proper management of the home was a surprisingly complex art: "There is more to be learned about pouring out tea and coffee, than most young ladies are willing to believe." *Godey's* went so far as to suggest coyly, in "Learning vs. Housewifery" that the two were complementary, not opposed: chemistry could be utilized in cooking, geometry in dividing cloth, and phrenology in discovering talent in children. . . .

. . . The female was dangerously addicted to novels, according to the literature of the period. She should avoid them, since they interfered with "serious piety." If she simply couldn't help herself and read them anyway, she should choose edifying ones from lists of morally acceptable authors. She should study history since it "showed the depravity of the human heart and the evil nature of sin." On the whole, "religious biography was best." . . .

No matter what later authorities claimed, the nineteenth century knew that girls *could* be ruined by a book. The seduction stories regard "exciting and dangerous books" as contributory causes of disaster. The man without honorable intentions always provides the innocent maiden with such books as a prelude to his assault on her virtue. Books which attacked or seemed to attack woman's accepted place in society were regarded as equally dangerous. A reviewer of Harriet Martineau's *Society in America* wanted it kept out of the hands of American women. They were so susceptible to persuasion, with their "gentle yielding natures" that they might listen to "the bold ravings of the hard-featured of their own sex." The frightening result: "such reading will unsettle them for their true station and pursuits, and they will throw the world back again into confusion." . . .

Most . . . advice was directed to woman as wife. Marriage was the proper state for the exercise of the domestic virtues. . . .

The corollary to marriage . . . was motherhood, which added another dimension to her usefulness and her prestige. It also anchored

her even more firmly to the home. "My Friend," wrote Mrs. Sigourney, "If in becoming a mother, you have reached the climax of
your happiness, you have also taken a higher place in the scale of
being . . . you have gained an increase of power." The Rev. J. N.
Danforth pleaded in *The Ladies' Casket,* "Oh, mother, acquit thyself
well in thy humble sphere, for thou mayest affect the world." A true
woman naturally loved her children; to suggest otherwise was monstrous.

America depended upon her mothers to raise up a whole generation of Christian statesmen who could say "all that I am I owe to my
angel mother." The mothers must do the inculcating of virtue since
the fathers, alas, were too busy chasing the dollar. Or as *The Ladies'
Companion* put it more effusively, the father "weary with the heat
and burden of life's summer day, or trampling with unwilling foot
the decaying leaves of life's autumn, has forgotten the sympathies
of life's joyous springtime. . . . The acquisition of wealth, the advancement of his children in worldly honor—these are his self-im-
posed tasks." It was his wife who formed "the infant mind as yet
untainted by contact with evil . . . like wax beneath the plastic hand
of the mother." . . .

If any woman asked for greater scope for her gifts the magazines
were sharply critical. Such women were tampering with society,
undermining civilization. Mary Wollstonecraft, Frances Wright and
Harriet Martineau were condemned in the strongest possible language—they were read out of the sex. "They are only semi-women,
mental hermaphrodites." The Rev. Harrington knew the women of
America could not possibly approve of such perversions and went
to some wives and mothers to ask if they did want a "wider sphere
of interest" as these nonwomen claimed. The answer was reassuring.
" '*No!*' they cried simultaneously, 'Let the men take care of politics,
we will take care of the children!' " Again female discontent resulted
only from a lack of understanding: women were not subservient, they
were rather "chosen vessels." Looked at in this light the conclusion
was inescapable: "Noble, sublime is the task of the American
mother." . . .

The American woman had her choice—she could define her rights
in the way of the women's magazines and insure them by the practice of the requisite virtues, or she could go outside the home, seek-

ing other rewards than love. It was a decision on which, she was told, everything in her world depended. "Yours it is to determine," the Rev. Mr. Stearns solemnly warned from the pulpit, "whether the beautiful order of society . . . shall continue as it has been" or whether "society shall break up and become a chaos of disjointed and unsightly elements." If she chose to listen to other voices than those of her proper mentors, sought other rooms than those of her home, she lost both her happiness and her power—"that almost magic power, which, in her proper sphere, she now wields over the destinies of the world."

But even while the women's magazines and related literature encouraged this ideal of the perfect woman, forces were at work in the nineteenth century which impelled woman herself to change, to play a more creative role in society. The movements for social reform, westward migration, missionary activity, utopian communities, industrialism, the Civil War—all called forth responses from woman which differed from those she was trained to believe were hers by nature and divine decree. The very perfection of True Womanhood, moreover, carried within itself the seeds of its own destruction. For if woman was so very little less than the angels, she should surely take a more active part in running the world, especially since men were making such a hash of things.

Real women often felt they did not live up to the ideal of True Womanhood: some of them blamed themselves, some challenged the standard, some tried to keep the virtues and enlarge the scope of womanhood. Somehow through this mixture of challenge and acceptance, of change and continuity, the True Woman evolved into the New Woman—a transformation as startling in its way as the abolition of slavery or the coming of the machine age. And yet the stereotype, the "mystique" if you will, of what woman was and ought to be persisted, bringing guilt and confusion in the midst of opportunity.

The women's magazines and related literature had feared this very dislocation of values and blurring of roles. By careful manipulation and interpretation they sought to convince woman that she had the best of both worlds—power and virtue—and that a stable order of society depended upon her maintaining her traditional place in it. To that end she was identified with everything that was beautiful and holy. . . .

Further Reading

As Professor Welter notes, her essay primarily makes use of women's magazines, gift books and religious literature; this material is not easily available to the undergraduate. There are, however, surveys of this literature, which can be consulted: Eleanor W. Thompson, *Education for Ladies, 1830–60: Ideas on Education in Magazines for Women* (New York, 1947); Anne Kuhn, *The Mother's Role in Childhood Education, New England Concepts 1830–60* (New Haven, 1947); Arthur Schlesinger, *Learning How to Behave: A Historical Study of American Etiquette Books* (New York, 1946); and Herbert R. Brown, *The Sentimental Novel in America, 1789–1860* (Durham, N.C., 1940). More specific studies include Keith Melder, "Ladies Bountiful: Organized Women's Benevolence in Early 19th-Century America," *New York History* (July, 1967), pp. 231–255; Welter, "Anti-Intellectualism and the American Woman: 1800–1860," *Mid-America* (October, 1966), pp. 258–270; and R. W. Hogeland, " 'The Female Appendage': Feminine Life-Styles in America, 1820–1860," *Civil War History* (June, 1971), pp. 101–114. For those interested in southern Womanhood during this period, see William R. Taylor, "The Plantation Becomes a Matriarchy," *Cavalier and Yankee: The Old South and American National Character* (New York, 1961), pp. 141–151; and Anne Firor Scott, *The Southern Lady: From Pedestal to Politics, 1830–1930* (Chicago, 1970), esp. Chapters 2 and 3.

Donald B. Meyer
THE TROUBLED SOULS OF FEMALES

Donald Meyer (b. 1923) is a graduate of Harvard University and teaches at Wesleyan University. What intrigues Meyer about the "positive thinkers," beginning with Mary Baker Eddy and other nineteenth-century advocates of "mind cure," is their attempt to systematically do away with consciousness and thereby avoid facing the demanding realities of life. Women joined the ranks of these partisans of mental tranquility in greater numbers than men. Why?

For Meyer the answer to this question is central to an understanding of male-female relationships. For the most part nineteenth-century men had little problem coming to terms with who they were, particularly after 1830 when they were in short supply everywhere in the United States. "A man was real to the extent that he moved," observes the author, "for motion registered his self-impulsion." It was this very criterion of male self-identification which caused women to have inner doubts about themselves. The more their men succeeded in the world of motion, the less middle- and upper-class women were needed economically. The more men worked, the less there was for women to do. Thus as American men became increasingly obsessed with work during the nineteenth century, and as earning money was equated with possessions, the obvious danger for women (since they were at home making no economic contribution) was that women themselves might become merely possessions. Professor Meyer further notes that this dilemma was compounded by the "ideology of mother," which made women accountable for the advancement of civilization while segregating them in the home. With their husbands absent for long periods of time, and aware of their meager knowledge of the outside world, how were women fit to raise sons, or save the world? Within this context it is little wonder that women made themselves sick and embraced "mind cure" as a way of getting well entirely within oneself, thus escaping the necessity of wrestling with the hard questions about being female.

Among several conspicuous features, perhaps the most obvious in the evangel of mind cure was the ubiquity of women. Not only was its most famous exponent a woman; scores of its lesser exponents were women, as founders, writers, preachers, teachers, healers. Mind cure gave jobs to women by hundreds and thousands. The clear majority of Christian Science practitioners were women. The majority of preachers in the proliferating Unity churches were to be women. Mind cure had higher proportions of women in its congregations than the old churches. Women bought its books heavily. Was there something wrong with women? . . .

The nineteenth century in the United States was a great age for men. Men were in short supply everywhere. De Tocqueville's portrait was that of a society where every (white) man fancied his life in terms of his "chances," and these were real. Once industry put down lasting roots and urban life began to spread, after 1830, practically every head and hand found welcome. There were opportunities for all sorts of businesses. Mechanics were needed, artisans, machinists and engineers. Men learned on the job. Most of the railroads were built sloppily, partly because of the priority of profit-lust, but partly because of the shortage of skill. Foremen were needed, and clerks. And expanding businessmen gradually realized they needed offices: managers, executives, administrators—and even salesmen—were needed. This was the dizziness of freedom, the dizziness of that mobility so impressive to European visitors. Banks sprang up like weeds. As agents and shepherds of every substantial interest, lawyers swarmed. A remarkable array of new identities, well-defined in terms of capital, skills, energy, role, advancement, presented itself everywhere. And incredibly, there were plenty of chances to drift, to float, to recover anonymity and start again, to escape, or at least to indulge the fantasy of escape. The whole nation was a West.

All this had been new. For most men, even into the early years of the nineteenth century, it had still been true that they knew themselves according to their place in a scheme of things, that of the village, of the parish, of the craft, overarched with appropriate cosmological myths. There was a whole of which they were a part, and the part found definition and integral standing in the whole. The new way, for the men of the nineteenth century, was to know oneself as potency, as power. A man was real to the extent that he moved, for motion registered his self-impulsion. One of the features of the age was the crumbling of old concepts of the whole. If there was a "scheme of things," it was much cloudier and less explicit than the schemes of the past. The immense self-consciousness that colonial Americans had invested in re-creating around themselves in an empty land the security of a stable solid social order was translated into the intense self-consciousness of individuals forging themselves as embodiments of Will. Excitement, clamor, room for aggression, a multitude of hard realities with which to grapple—men had these to enjoy.

Women in the nineteenth century were not so lucky. Some were not lucky at all. Of course, for the large majority of women life remained, almost through the century, reasonably close to what it had been. A woman's duties on the farm remained clear—though even farm women began to suffer: mechanization of farm work, for instance, was in the first place mechanization of the man's work more than of the woman's; and, by comparison with the new urban glamour, the farm woman could come to feel herself doomed to lonely drudgery. Were Grange socials enough? Still, in countless small towns women continued to exercise all-round craftsmanship. And in both scenes, there were hardly more confusions in the roles of wife and mother than had always haunted these supremely subtle destinies.

But the women of the future were the women whose men were caught up in the new world of motion. The situation such women faced had its frustrating simplicity. The more their men succeeded, the less they were needed. The more their husbands worked, the less they had to work. In an age of vast demands upon manpower, a small but growing quantity of womanpower was neglected. The farmer and his wife had been a work-team; so also the wife and her husband in the self-sufficient monopolistic small towns. But just what did the middle-class female contribute?

The Busyness of the Victorian Housewife

One solution to underemployment was make-work. Compared to the efficient simplicities of older abodes, the middle-class home took on complication. Those older simplicities often enough testified to a plain—though relative—poverty, which a seasoned asceticism took in stride. Yet, one of the telling things about the new affluence was that it did not after all achieve comfort. Instead, from the eighteen-thirties and then blatantly in the Victorian household of the postwar generation, the domestic environment grew crowded, stuffed with a welter of furniture, each piece itself curled and carved, with folds and hangings and ruffles appended everywhere. Everything caught a great deal of dust—and then had to be dusted. The various theaters of male existence—office, courtroom, factory, livery stable—got no cleaner; some were willfully dirty. Cleanliness meant home. The nineteenth-century Protestant estimate of cleanliness as next to godliness reflected something more than an appreciation of the new scientific hygiene; it reflected a search for something to do. The woman who kept busy keeping her home clean worked hard, but the meaning of the work was veiled. Besides, with supplies of Irish, then Swedish and German and other immigrant girls abundant, often enough it was the maid who dusted anyway.

Simply to know what sofas, what tables, what lamps and hangings and *objets d'art,* what silver to buy was a job, naturally. Indeed, simply to know how to go about practically anything became a matter for a higher level of awareness and study. How to dress, how to eat, what to eat, what to read, what to feel, how to behave at parties, what styles and—soon—what brands to buy: such nagging uncertainties supported a genre of books, manuals, newspapers, magazines, almanacs. Clearly indebted to the Puritan determination to be disciplined and under control in all things, in the nineteenth century this quest for advice broke free from Puritan motives in favor of new ones.

They were complex, these new motives. The use of styles and manners to exhibit one's elevated status was hardly disguised, and the career of that conspicuous consuming made notorious by Thorstein Veblen had entered its democratic phase, confined no longer (as Veblen never thoroughly realized, his capacity for revulsion being only human and therefore limited) to the distinctly predatory. Though Veblen indicated that the purpose of conspicuous displays was to display one's freedom from the servitude of work, one must observe against him that few men—few males, that is—actually did stop work. Work—in the twentieth century it was to be called a "game"—had become an obsession. As for women, conspicuous consumption, whether on the level of the most marginal or on that of Fifth Avenue, occupied them closer to the heart. If it in one way signaled a woman's freedom from one sort of labor, it also gave her another job. The career of the woman whose busyness is shopping had begun. Man earns, woman spends.

Changing Virtues

In earlier times the basic virtues praised and rewarded by the community, in the voice of its Protestant conscience, had been acceptably distinct. Following the more precisely religious qualities of humility, a repenting heart, subscription to various theological truths, and often some charity, these virtues had included the useful traits of the Protestant, Calvinist, Puritan ethic: diligence, frugality, honesty. These had been incumbent upon everyone; that is, they were expected of man and woman alike. For both, they were advantageous, serving as a sufficiently complete portrait of basic character on the frontier, on the farm, in the villages and towns still unchallenged by change, machines and mobility. Between the farmhouse and the fields, between the shop and the home, there obtained no functional contrast in styles of human being. . . .

. . . In the new culture, home and family were supported by a man making money. Money was translated into possessions. The woman, at home, making no money, ran an obvious danger. Woman herself might become a possession. One can find in the biographies of eminent female reformers evidence of their instinct to escape possession on most intimate levels—in their debt to emancipated fathers, in their marriage to younger men, in their not marrying at all, in their criticism of wifehood and motherhood, even in an unconventional occasional reversal of the order of marriage and motherhood. Not to become reflexive, not to be simply the object and evidence of wishes outside themselves—this was a distinct concern. . . .

The Danger of Enslavement

. . . Their usefulness having become ambiguous, women faced the danger of being turned into possessions, hence enslaved and passive. The escape that took form as a leading model for female existence for some forty years tried to finesse the danger. Women were superior. A female existence radically different from that of men, different in its inner organization, its refinement, its transcendence above the hard materials of the world, became a style for those who could afford it. In its prewar naïveté, full of romantic sensibility, it had the virtue of being new at least, hence something yet to be explored; ' in its postwar routine of respectable gentility, it bred exhaustion. To obey these ascriptions of special qualities, women had more to do than just accept tradition. They had to forget and to pretend. They had to convince themselves, to will themselves to be creatures without will.

The primary arena of decision was obvious. For thirty years before the Civil War, discussion had swirled around the family in all its aspects—kitchen, nursery, sitting room, clothes closet, and of course bedroom. Not that such self-consciousness was new. The earliest Puritans landing on American shores had been forced to sharp awareness of the family order, but this had been part of a general awareness and anxiety. In order to avert disintegration in the wilderness they had had to calculate policy for everything, church and state, economy and education, and leisure as well, the family drawing no especially obsessed attention. In the nineteenth century the family did draw particular regard.

It seemed possible that the family might prove to be the central bulwark of stability and values. Not the family but everything else was disintegrating and the family therefore at all costs must hold. This sense was particularly evident in the old denominations of classic Puritan descent. Protestantism itself appeared to be disintegrating into a welter of sects; religious authority crumbled; the prestige of the ministry crumbled. In the accelerating democratization of society, established economic and social and political authority crumbled, and political struggles to save them seemed doomed. Upon the family, then, let trust for stability in the flux be loaded. Puritanism had never dreamed of entrusting it so much.

This intensified responsibility, moreover, ran in the face of the continuing assumption by outside agencies of old duties of the home. The nineteenth century saw the spread at last of a public school system. Factories were beginning to produce what had commonly been made at home. Popular reading and entertainment were beginning to supply what the family circle had long supplied. Becoming more specialized, the family at the same time was expected to become more influential. . . .

The Ideology of Mother

What really mobilized the logic of the saving family was . . . the more specialized ideology of mother. Tirelessly celebrated in New England and the East before the Civil War, mother was revealed as the key figure in civilization. Holy being of total virtue, calm and elevated substance, and perfect comprehension of her children, mother constituted a role in obvious compensation for losses. Though fewer than those of her predecessors, the tasks of the new-model mother

were more intense. In order to radiate the high moral and psychological traits entrusted to her for inculcation, she had to enjoy a
higher estimate of her meaning. In order to specialize in psychological affairs, she had to become a more purely internal creature.

When integrated into a spreading liberal Protestant preoccupation
with love as the supreme expression of religious reality, and with
"personality" as the highest form of existence, this reevaluation of
mother secreted genuine potentials for an emotional generosity and
a fine carelessness in life which the old faith and the old culture
had rarely stressed and frequently suppressed. But these potentials
found precious little expression, for the way the job was conceived
carried its obvious corollary. Women were to be segregated. Ideal
mother simply intensified the notion of a normative female character
generated in the new classes, and taken over from England, which
always meant that that character required its special circumstances,
its carefully defined environment, its strict boundaries, that it might
flourish.

In this ideology success bred failure. The very virtues of the ideal
woman and mother unfitted her for one of her jobs. Upon half her
children her influence could have been suitable—upon her girls.
But for preparing her boys she was incompetent, assuming that her
boys were in fact to "leave home." Protected from the world precisely in order to conserve her special attributes, she knew nothing
of it. Boys raised by pure women might never gain competence in
the world of hard knocks. . . .

Popular social myth reflected this maladaptation of the moral
middle-class family well on into the twentieth century. The boyhood
appropriate to the man who succeeded in the world of hard knocks
remained that of the older world of the farms and the small towns,
as though only here, not in the comfortable-uncomfortable gentility
of respectable urban-suburban families did the male gain that fundamental conditioning he needed. Contrary to the notion of mother as
cause, the man of success vaunted himself as his own cause; he
"made" himself; he was the "self-made" man of endless fraternal
oratory.

The Fatherless Best-Sellers

. . . Consigned to segregated delicacy, women consumed—and hence
inspired—a vast literature for women, by women, about women. Long

neglected as innocently trivial fodder for innocently private lives, this literature yields, upon inspection, somewhat unnerving contents. Reading through from Susan Warner's *Wide Wide World* of 1850, to such best-sellers as Eleanor Porter's *Pollyanna* of 1913, including, Louisa May Alcott's *Little Women* of 1868, and Kate Wiggins' *Rebecca of Sunnybrook Farm* of 1903, one is, if attentive, somewhat puzzled by a consistent vacuum. Father is missing. He is missing psychologically because he is inept, not a father at all, as in *Little Women,* or he is lost, or he is dead. Evidently, for the female authors to present their female readers an image of the independent, self-responsible girl (such as the charming Jo), the presence of the generative male had to be dispensed with. As for other levels, Beatrice Hofstadter, recently rereading more of the impeccably moral lady-novelists of the age, has clearly shown the underlying wish of so many delectable heroines. Once she has identified the man she means to marry, the heroine turns to making him over (as, appallingly, father could not be made over). He must be tamed. He must be, as the heroine of Augusta Evans Wilson's novel *St. Elmo* (1867) sets out to assure, emasculated. In these phantasmic basements of popular culture, one finds opposites meaning the same thing. In *Virgin Land,* Henry Nash Smith has described the transvestite appearance, from the seventies, of the lady gunmen in dime Westerns, shooting, swearing, smoking, drinking—and worse..

It is hard to be surprised. The repression being imposed in the fifties and nailed down in the seventies was a special pathology, not the discipline of a long-seasoned long-practiced style but a defensive, emergency, improvised ideology. Women, as the old Puritan refusal to preach any less severe a doctrine to women and children than to men recognized, had a life in the real world. How could the instinct for reality be repressed? In her ideal guise, all the woman's special attributes, all her assignment to her special sphere, bespoke one thing: she was weak, standing in this weakness at the furthest remove from the basic image of male existence as potency and power, self-sufficiency and will. Men had their own passion, and at the prospect of emancipated women recoiled with that fright special to those addicted to an obsession. Not a single reform, not even the obviously humane progress of medicine, failed to evoke male hysteria, often that of ministers themselves. Anesthesia in childbirth was "against nature," female education was against nature;

bloomers—pre-Civil War slacks—were against nature. Natural, normative, respectable female existence decreed the passivity and weakness of women. In that event, where was salvation but in demanding a world for the weak? Weak, women could not maintain themselves in their own proper image even when (and this was probably most of the time) they wanted to. Things began to go wrong with them. What then if passivity could be strength?

Naturally there were many paths. Nor could the segregated enjoy an undisturbed fruition. Supposedly both exalted and weak, some women, an adventurous few, might insist that elevation deserved strength, and go into charity and social work. Fewer might deny the myth of two realms altogether, entering the male's world of careers, or even of free imagination. Others might find in woman's world the ferocities of "Society" slaking competitive energies as surely as the economy, or a renewed realism about the family circle itself, about children, and about men and women together. And there were plenty of signs of impatience, toward the end of the nineteenth century, with narrowness of life, among men as well, free enough, imaginative enough, strong enough to wish for variety, new things, new devotions. The gay nineties could not, after all, have been so gay had not the essentials of its gaiety been ready—men and women both, boys and girls together.

Through the history of the race, deeper in time than historians usually tell, one thing most of all has offered relief from dilemmas: keeping busy. But among all mothers, among all women, some especially were badly off. Life as mother was short. As fewer children were born, as medicine added years, the job of processing children comprised a smaller and smaller fraction of the lifeline. What happened when a woman was fifty-five? Or fifty? Or forty-five? In the old days old age still had its family place. In the old family even the occasional spinster, just as the widowed grandmother (or grandfather), still worked and ruled. With the new ways of mobility a new organization of age had evolved: each generation for itself. The measureless and dreadful loneliness of senior citizens, retirement, biological and familial superannuation, portended. For women it arrived first and worst. Forty-five or fifty was not so old; a woman might be at the peak of her personal (as distinguished from her biologically maternal) powers. Men were supposed to be at that age. What filled the void? "Sham emotions," as Miss Call called them, were alluring. And through these sham emotions a woman could get sick. She could make herself sick. Though she was exalted, something was wrong; but though something was wrong, she was weak. To be sick was a route for the pure but weak, neither the masterful, aggressive reform of reality by the strong nor the anarchic selfish rebellion of the weak and impure. To make oneself sick was an escape, for it invited a project which at the same time did not require one to wrestle with the world. Perhaps the world meant no malice. Perhaps the world, despite one's own debility, was friendly. Perhaps it was only the faulty imagination within oneself that inhibited one's enjoyment of a harmonic universe. The project of getting well could be pursued entirely within oneself.

Further Reading

There are few sources that deal directly with the dilemma women faced in the second half of the nineteenth century as described by Professor Meyer. A starting point for surveying the general subject of male-female relationships is Sidney H. Ditzion, *Marriage, Morals and Sex in America: A History of Ideas* (New York, 1953); and Leslie A. Fiedler, *Love and Death in the American Novel* (New York, 1960). Two studies specifically devoted to the inquiry are William Wasserstrom, *Heiress of All the Ages: Sex and Sentiment in the Genteel Tradition* (Minneapolis, 1959); and G. J. Barker-Benfield, "The Spermatic Economy: A Nineteenth-Century View of Sexuality," *Feminist Studies* (Summer, 1972). A somewhat similar approach is applied by William R. Taylor and Christopher Lasch, "Two 'Kindred Spirits': Sorority and Family in New England, 1839–1846," *New England Quarterly* (March, 1963), pp. 23–41; and see also Ronald W. Hogeland, "Co-education of the Sexes at Oberlin College: A Study of Social Ideas in Mid-Nineteenth-Century America," *Journal of Social History* (Winter, 1972–1973), pp. 160–176, for the earlier period.

IV TWENTIETH-CENTURY AMERICAN LIFE

Conflicting Opinions

The following selections explore twentieth-century American opinions about the definition of womanhood. The remarks of Mrs. Burton Harrison, self-proclaimed conservative, and Dr. Benjamin Spock, militant radical, are curiously similar. Both consider female Americans as possessing an innate, peculiar nature that irrevocably ties them to the domestic sphere and child-rearing. Reminiscent of nineteenth-century domestic reformer Catharine Beecher, Harrison and Spock believe that if women insist upon seeking fulfillment outside of the home, dire consequences will ensue for the society as well as for women. In contrast, Charlotte Perkins Gilman and Frances Beal understand womanhood as not limited by the submissive/passive model of being "feminine," nor do they believe that women's role need be confined to the domestic domain. As Gilman argues, since women are persons they have the capacity to participate in a wide range of activities that express their humanity without becoming "masculine." This opportunity should, of course, extend to black women; yet it rarely has. According to black activist Frances Beal, the problem of being a black woman in America is compounded by pressures both from emerging black manhood and from white society to become, or remain, submissive.

Mrs. Burton Harrison

HOME LIFE AS A PROFESSION (1900)

Today, when hundreds of young women of our best blood and culture in America are standing within the open doors of schools and colleges, eagerly straining their gaze out into the future, hoping to catch a glimpse of the opportunity for a "career," it seems to behoove the conservative thinkers among us to suggest to some of them the profession of home life. This is not meant to apply to those whom exceptional talent and ability have bidden to especial callings. They are as sure to find their vocations and to succeed in them as smoke is to fly upward. My modest suggestions are intended rather for the rank and file of clever, ambitious, well-educated girls who in this epoch of the world's advance feel that they are born for higher things than the drudgery to which they consider their mothers' lives to have been sacrificed. If they contemplate marriage at all, it is as an accident, not a destiny. They do not desire to walk side by side with man, but ahead of him.

Now, as a matter of historic fact, the cornerstone of the highest civilization has always been the home, and wifehood and motherhood the happiest estate of woman. To my mind, it is a cruel wrong to a young girl to launch her in life unadvised on these points, and imbued with the determination to independence of the other sex. Sooner or later she must find herself possessed of the strong feminine yearning to rest her burdens upon shoulders broader than her own; to surrender into larger hands her ability to battle successfully with fate; to let herself be cared for and cherished; to taste the exalted joy of having the beings she has given to the world look to her for their best happiness and inspiration. What if disappointment, if disillusionment, the sorrows of a common lot, fall to her share? She will have lived and loved! No reward of intellectual supremacy, no winning of money on her own account, no plaudits of lookers-on bestowed upon her achievements of brain and energy, could atone to her for the lack of that simple elemental experience, old as the world, apportioned to Eve's daughters all alike! And no amount of previous witty scoffing at the monster man, the oppressor of her sex, will save her from the risk of someday wanting to encounter it.

From *Harper's Bazar*, Vol. 33 (May 19, 1900).

This opinion has been reached not through exhaustive study of the introduction of women into the professions and industrial life, but rather after observation of the inner history of many of the sisterhood of brain-workers who have successfully solved the problem under discussion. More than a few of these have said to me, "I would give up all I have gained tomorrow, if I could be sure of the loving shelter of a good husband's care." It is this kind of woman who, if she marries at all, is apt to do so only when assured of the highest and most thorough companionship; and as that desideratum is not easily attainable in the world of everyday, the chance of her marriage is small. Hence the cultivated, largely developed feminine intellect goes in general into devoting itself to the enlightenment of other people's children; and to the little, loving, trusting, unquestioning average woman is left the sweet and sacred duty of rearing and influencing her own. If, as a wise man said, "women are made and meant to be not men, but the mothers of men," it is a great loss to the future of our country when the clever and accomplished girl sets out in life with the deliberate purpose of carving out her own destiny unaided. She is often actually so busy thinking of man as a competitor, she has no time to consider him as a comrade, still less a lover or husband.

Far be it from me to suggest a relapse to those dark ages of home life when a girl strummed on the piano or worked in crossstitch tapestry what time she was not engaged in dressing or receiving "beaux," until she married and passed into a new arena. On the contrary, I would have her carry back into her home her sheaves of knowledge and accomplishment, and there try to enrich and broaden the domestic sphere. The refreshment of such companionship as hers to her tired elders would be like adding a new span to their lives. Her loving ministry to their needs, her fresh words of thought applied to their "commonplace" topics, her information and culture injected into their "humdrum" conversation, would make even an adverse turn of Fortune's wheel endurable. But to too many girls this field of action seems less interesting than grappling with outside objects that demand their zeal and learning. Often the vista of home life, as they look back down the years before their emancipation from it, presents nothing inspiring them to effort. Ever since they can remember they have seen their mothers more or less borne down with petty cares, petty ailments, petty fault-findings from those for whom they are toiling. What "opportunity" does that sort of a life present for the development of exalted latter-day ambitions? Rather does she think, with a sudden inflation of the soul, of this chance to escape from an atmosphere where such conditions are unavoidable. It will be so grand to live free as man, in the heart of a great city, feeling nothing of the mosquito pricks of housekeeping and family cares, allowing the diviner part of her to soar into the ether of high endeavor, and testing by wages earned the value of her brain-power. Nothing in her mother's lot of having and bringing up children, of creating a home, of being the universal sympathizer and referee of a many-minded family, appeals to her fastidious sense. The idea of a husband who will thwart and restrain her ambitions possesses no attraction. If what she sees be all the reward her mother has gained for such an immense output of strength, patience, and devotion, why need she fash herself to follow the domestic path? . . .

. . . In old days women were fitted only for housewives, with an added smattering of poor English, worse French, and such "accomplishments" as the grace of Heaven soon enabled them to forget. Now we go to the other extreme, and allow our daughters of the cultured class of society no privileges of honest information about homely indispensables. Indeed, the days of their early youth are all too short for the amount of mental and physical training deemed necessary to their education. Kindergarten, day school, boarding school, and college absorb the chief part of their first sixteen or eighteen years of existence, and the holidays are taken up with special lessons or in travelling abroad. Household machinery is, to the majority of them, almost as much of a mystery as the workings of a steam engine. . . .

The painful truth is that home life in our busy day and generation is passing out of vogue. Even where the daughters are not examples of high intellectual accomplishment, each one has her fad or mission, keeping her for hours abroad, or else when indoors bent over a desk heaped with notes to answer, minutes to be made up, reports to be prepared for the printer, or papers to be written for the next meeting of her association of similar devotees. At breakfast she is too absorbed in tearing open and digesting her correspondence to be able to diffuse around her the aroma of gracious and sympathizing young womanhood which would help to arm the men of the family for their fight with circumstance downtown. At dinner she is

FIGURE 5. The gap between the rhetoric about motherhood and the reality of the conditions which many women faced, is no more vividly portrayed than in the plight of working women at the turn of the twentieth century. *(State Historical Society of Wisconsin)*

again brimful of affairs, consulting her father and brothers upon matters of law and real estate that have come up for settlement in her committee. Her fair young brow is perpetually puckered with considerations of business and administration. She is too utterly preoccupied with these concerns to take upon herself the minor responsibility of enlivening a set of jaded males, who, once within their own doors, desire never to hear of her favorite topics.

We American women all take our "public works" too seriously, toil and strive too unremittingly, give too little heed to the trivial round of home life, which we expect to maintain itself unaided. The girls who are coming on are better equipped than their mothers in the science of law and government. What they accomplish is often thoroughly well done, and deserving of highest praise, its results far-reaching in human society. In these matters, however, they might well take pattern by some young women, married and single, of highest rank in British aristocracy. Few of these great ladies are satisfied to sit with folded hands and enjoy their wealth and state. They read, write essays and speeches, mix in politics and social science, are forever on the wing apparently, yet for the greater part of the year one knows of them as working among the poor on their own estates, interesting themselves in cookery, sanitation of dwellings, gardening, clothing clubs, home book clubs, and so on, along the whole line of necessaries for the development of home life. Whether they are more expert than we in the economy of time and effort, or whether their climate and unhurrying habit of life befriend them, certain it is that this class of women in England and Scotland and Ireland look younger and fresher than their sisters over here. I feel sure that we too might attain that gratifying result, were it more customary with us, as with them, to make home the supreme center of life—to undertake it as a profession. . . .

I do not think our homes as they are now a sufficiently satisfying exchange for the broader, more interesting channels for women's work everywhere available. But I earnestly wish they might be made so; and the question of how to accomplish this enormously important result lies largely in the palm of the girl graduate of today.

Charlotte Perkins Gilman
ARE WOMEN HUMAN BEINGS? (1912)

. . . The male of our species, from the beginning of his power of conscious thought, has arrogated to himself as part of his sex the major attributes of humanity: religion, education, government, commerce—these were for him alone. In what he has termed "his female" he has seen, and for the most part still sees, only her femininity, never her humanity.

That she should concentrate all her human faculties upon the fulfilment of her feminine functions he has held quite right and proper; that she should at any time wish to use them, not as a female, but as a human being, is to him monstrous. So absolute has been this monopolization of human functions by one sex; so complete this obsession that has persisted in considering them as sex attributes, that even the range of industries originated by women, for ages practiced wholly by women, have been gradually absorbed by men, and as rapidly as they were absorbed have become "masculine."

Mere extension in method has been similarly classified: as where a woman with distaff and spindle, or foot-run wheel, was considered feminine; but to run a woolen mill must be "man's work."

Let us look at our own race history. When we were all hunters, fishers, and root-gatherers, we were men and women; just as efficiently and completely as we are now. When we kept cattle we were not any the less, or more, men and women. When we developed agriculture, we were still men and women. When we specialized in industry, we remained men and women. Men were males and women females at any time in the whole long story.

But while remaining unchanged in these respects, we have changed enormously in our social features, our common human attributes.

Specialization has given us a thousand trades, arts, crafts, and professions. Organization has multiplied our power myriad-fold. Invention and discovery have enriched and enlightened the world. Religions have changed. Governments have changed. Society evolves

From *Harper's Weekly*, Vol. 56 (May 25, 1912). For a more detailed discussion of this theme by the author consult *The Man-Made World or Our Androcentric Culture* (New York, 1911), esp. pp. 9–25.

from age to age. All these are human processes. They belong to our race. They are common to both male and female. They have no faintest connection with any sex distinction.

As to warfare, which our ultra males are so sure to fall back on in proof of their essential dominance; warfare is not a social process at all, but a social disease, freely admitted to be most characteristic of the male. It is the instinct of sex-combat, overdeveloped and mis-used.

The women of our age in most countries of the same degree of development are outgrowing the artificial restrictions so long placed upon them, and following natural lines of human advance. They are specializing, because they are human. They are organizing, because they are human. They are seeking economic and political independence, because they are human. They are demanding the vote, because they are human.

Against this swelling tide stands the mere mass of inert old-world ignorance, backed by the perverse misconception of modern minds, which even science fails to illuminate.

"Go back," says this mass. "You are women. You are nothing *but* women. You are females—nothing *but* females. All these things you want to do are male things. You cannot do them without being a male. You want to be males. It is abhorrent, outrageous, impossible!"

All these adjectives and horrors would be freely granted if women really could become males—or even if they wanted to! But what needs to be hammered into these male-ridden minds is that these things the women want to do and be and have are not in any sense masculine. They do not belong to men. They never did. They are departments of our social life, hitherto monopolized by men, but no more made masculine by that use than the wearing of trousers by Turkish women makes trousers feminine or the wearing of corsets by German officers makes corsets masculine. . . .

Whether in the accumulated literature of the necessarily unenlightened past, or the still accumulating literature of the wilfully unenlightened present, we find everywhere this same pervasive error, this naive assumption, which would be so insolent if it were not so absurd, that only men are human creatures, able and entitled to perform the work of the world; while women are only female creatures, able to do nothing whatever but continue in the same round of duties to which they have been so long restricted.

They darkly threaten, do these ultra-male opponents, that if women persist in doing human things they will lose the respect of man— yea, more, they will lose his pecuniary support.

They should study their biology a little more profoundly. The respect of the male for the female is based on the distinction of sex, not on political or economic disability. Men respect women because they are females, not because they are weak and ignorant and defenseless.

Women will never cease to be females, but they will cease to be weak and ignorant and defenseless. They are becoming wiser, stronger, better able to protect themselves, one another, and their children. Courage, power, achievement are always respected.

As women grow, losing nothing that is essential to womanhood, but adding steadily the later qualities of humanness, they will win and hold a far larger, deeper reverence than that hitherto vouch- safed them. As they so rise and broaden, filling their full place in the world as members of society, as well as their partial places as mothers of it, they will gradually rear a new race of men, men with minds large enough to see in human beings something besides males and females. . . .

Benjamin Spock
PROBLEMS OF SEX AND SEX ROLE

. . . The view that women are essentially the same as men has been accepted by an ever larger proportion of American women, without their stopping to realize what a revolutionary concept it is, or even being aware that people have not always thought this way. When I have lectured in universities and have referred to the differ- ences between the sexes in temperaments and satisfactions, young women have come up afterwards to ask incredulously whether they heard me correctly.

From *Decent and Indecent: Our Personal and Political Behavior,* pp. 44, 46–47, 56– 57. Copyright © 1969, 1970 by James M. Houston, Trustee, under an Irrevocable Trust dated October 6, 1966, between Benjamin M. Spock of Cleveland, Ohio, Donor, and James M. Houston of Pittsburgh, Pennsylvania, Trustee. Reprinted by permission of McCall Books, a Division of Saturday Review Press.

The main harm from the assumption of sameness is that it encourages an exaggerated rivalry that, I think, impairs the happiness of both sexes and the harmony between them. . . .

The proportion of women who are competitive with men is higher among those who have been to college, I believe, though I have no figures to prove this. I'm thinking not only about obvious rivalry in job preference and job performance. I'm thinking of the less visible differences that a man feels in talking socially or dealing occupationally with a woman who has the constant itch to argue and criticize, however subtly, and with a woman who accepts him comfortably as he is.

Today girls show a greater aggressiveness in sexual advances. This was brought out in the spontaneous comments of college students and faculty in several recent studies of sexual behavior: Girls themselves complain of how much sexual initiative they often have to take. Faculty people report their surprise at what a large proportion of the provocation and advances they happen to see is now initiated by girls. When recently I talked to an audience of college men on a different subject and referred casually to my impression that our culture is encouraging young women to be overly aggressive toward men, there was sudden vehement applause, much more than greeted anything else I said.

To some moderns this sexual boldness of girls seems like a wholesome change. They feel that men in past times asserted, without justification, a monopoly right to sexual initiative. This sounds plausible; but to me it ignores the temperamental differences between the sexes. I believe women are designed in their deepest instincts to get more pleasure out of life—not only sexually but socially, occupationally, maternally—when they are not aggressive. To put it another way I think that when women are encouraged to be competitive too many of them become disagreeable. I remember an article by a golf professional who expressed his consternation at the behavior of a third of the women who play the game at a typical club. They respond to the competition, he said, with conduct toward each other that ranges from arrogant to brazenly dishonest. It's not that men have nobler characters. It's that men are designed and reared to compete but also to keep their competitiveness disciplined within conventional bounds.

When a woman refrains from competing with men, or when a woman is gentle in manner, this doesn't mean that she has to be submissive. She has her sphere, her power, her expertness, her indispensability (if she's any good), her self-respect and the respect that she can demand from men. The person who thinks that to escape domination a woman must have 50 percent equality—quantitatively and qualitatively—has fallen into the trap of thinking always in terms of competition, as if woman is always in a race with man and must be exactly even or ahead or ignominiously behind. I'd say that man and woman are meant to be on separate roads, however close, not racing; and that on the occasions when their roads might cross, one defers at one time, the other at another, depending on the practical and ceremonial requirements. . . .

The subject of jobs for women is complex and controversial. A man who offers his opinion on it is asking for trouble, but I have to include mine in order to round out my theme. . . .

Women, I believe, should be able to get any kind of training they want and have an equal chance with men to get any jobs they want, at equal pay, including those jobs requiring a high degree of aggressiveness when that is their dish.

On the other hand I feel that since women have an inborn aptitude for—and naturally get gratification from—understanding and helping people and creating beauty, and since most of them are going to spend fifteen to twenty-five years of their lives primarily raising their children, it would be fairer to them if they were brought up at home and educated at school and college in such a spirit that they would enjoy, feel proud of, and be fascinated by child-rearing rather than frustrated by it. Then they would be less inclined to be rivalrous with their husbands and other men. If they sought outside jobs, they would prefer those that are compatible with feminine drives, for example, as nurses, social workers, teachers, librarians, designers and merchandizers of clothes, secretaries, physicians, psychologists, writers, actresses, architects, and decorators. And if they had careers in medicine or architecture, for instance, they should be able to make distinctly feminine contributions to the advancement of these fields, rather than compete with men in the usual manly traditions of these professions.

Frances Beal

DOUBLE JEOPARDY:
TO BE BLACK AND FEMALE

In attempting to analyze the situation of the black woman in America, one crashes abruptly into a solid wall of grave misconceptions, outright distortions of fact, and defensive attitudes on the part of many. . . .

The ideal model that is projected for a woman is to be surrounded by hypocritical homage and estranged from all real work, spending idle hours primping and preening, obsessed with conspicuous consumption, and limiting life's functions to simply a sex role. We unqualitatively reject these respective models. A woman who stays at home caring for children and the house often leads an extremely sterile existence. She must lead her entire life as a satellite to her mate. He goes out into society and brings back a little piece of the world for her. His interests and his understanding of the world become her own and she cannot develop herself as an individual having been reduced to only a biological function. This kind of woman leads a parasitic existence that can aptly be described as legalized prostitution.

Furthermore it is idle dreaming to think of black women simply caring for their homes and children like the middle-class white model. Most black women have to work to help house, feed, and clothe their families. Black women make up a substantial percentage of the black working force, and this is true for the poorest black family as well as the so-called "middle-class" family.

Black women were never afforded any such phony luxuries. Though we have been browbeaten with this white image, the reality of the degrading and dehumanizing jobs that were relegated to us quickly dissipated this mirage of womanhood. The following excerpts from a speech that Sojourner Truth made at a Women's Rights Convention in the nineteenth century show us how misleading and incomplete a life this model represents for us:

> . . . Well, chilern, whar dar is so much racket dar must be something out o' kilter. I tink dat 'twixt de niggers of de Souf and de women at de Norf all a talkin' 'bout rights, de white men will be in a fix pretty soon. But what's all dis here talkin' 'bout? Dat man ober dar say dat women needs to be helped into carriages, and lifted ober ditches, and to have de best place every whar. Nobody ever help me into carriages, or ober mud puddles, or gives me any best places, . . . and ar'nt I a woman? Look at me! Look at my arm! . . . I have plowed, and planted, and gathered into barns, and no man could head me—and ar'nt I a woman? I could work as much as a man (when I could get it), and bear de lash as well—and ar'nt I a woman? I have borne five chilern and I seen 'em mos' all sold off into slavery, and when I cried out with a mother's grief, none but Jesus heard—and ar'nt I a woman?

Unfortunately, there seems to be some confusion in the Movement today as to who has been oppressing whom. Since the advent of black power, the black male has exerted a more prominent leadership role in our struggle for justice in this country. He sees the system for what it really is for the most part, but where he rejects its values and mores on many issues, when it comes to women, he seems to take his guidelines from the pages of the *Ladies' Home Journal.* Certain black men are maintaining that they have been castrated by society but that black women somehow escaped this persecution and even contributed to this emasculation.

Let me state here and now that the black woman in America can justly be described as a "slave of a slave." By reducing the black man in America to such abject oppression, the black woman had no protector and was used, and is still being used in some cases, as the scapegoat for the evils that this horrendous system has perpetrated on black men. Her physical image has been maliciously maligned; she has been sexually molested and abused by the white colonizer; she has suffered the worst kind of economic exploitation, having been forced to serve as the white woman's maid and wet nurse for white offspring while her own children were more often than not starving and neglected. It is the depth of degradation to be socially manipulated, physically raped, used to undermine your own household, and to be powerless to reverse this syndrome.

It is true that our husbands, fathers, brothers, and sons have been emasculated, lynched, and brutalized. They have suffered from the cruelest assault on mankind that the world has ever known. However, it is a gross distortion of fact to state that black women have op-

FIGURE 6. Black womanhood has never fit America's "feminine ideal." Black women have come more recently to discover their own historic roots. *(Leo and Diane Dillon)*

pressed black men. The capitalist system found it expedient to en-
slave and oppress them and proceeded to do so without consultation
or the signing of any agreements with black women.

It must also be pointed out at this time that black women are not
resentful of the rise to power of black men. We welcome it. We see in
it the eventual liberation of all black people from this corrupt system
of capitalism. Nevertheless, this does not mean that you have to
negate one for the other. This kind of thinking is a product of mis-
education; that it's either X or it's Y. It is fallacious reasoning that in
order for the black man to be strong, the black woman has to be
weak.

Those who are exerting their "manhood" by telling black women
to step back into a domestic, submissive role are assuming a counter-
revolutionary position. Black women likewise have been abused by
the system and we must begin talking about the elimination of all
kinds of oppression. If we are talking about building a strong nation,
capable of throwing off the yoke of capitalist oppression, then we
are talking about the total involvement of every man, woman, and
child, each with a highly developed political consciousness. We need
our whole army out there dealing with the enemy and not half an
army.

There are also some black women who feel that there is no more
productive role in life than having and raising children. This attitude
often reflects the conditioning of the society in which we live and is
adopted from a bourgeois white model. Some young sisters who have
never had to maintain a household and accept the confining role
which this entails tend to romanticize (along with the help of a few
brothers) this role of housewife and mother. Black women who have
had to endure this kind of function are less apt to have these
utopian visions.

Those who project in an intellectual manner how great and rewarding this role will be and who feel that the most important thing that
they can contribute to the black nation is children are doing themselves a great injustice. This line of reasoning completely negates the
contributions that black women have historically made to our struggle for liberation. These black women include Sojourner Truth,
Harriet Tubman, Mary McLeod Bethune, and Fannie Lou Hamer, to
name but a few.

We live in a highly industrialized society and every member of the black nation must be as academically and technologically developed as possible. To wage a revolution, we need competent teachers, doctors, nurses, electronics experts, chemists, biologists, physicists, political scientists, and so on and so forth. Black women sitting at home reading bedtime stories to their children are just not going to make it.

Critique

David M. Kennedy
THE NINETEENTH-CENTURY HERITAGE: THE FAMILY, FEMINISM AND SEX

"By the end of the nineteenth century it was becoming increasingly difficult to contain real women within the myth of the feminine ideal," asserts David Kennedy (b. 1941) of Stanford University. The following excerpt from his book on the career of Margaret Sanger serves as a penetrating analysis of the predicament American women faced at the turn of the century as they attempted to deal with the question of who they really were.*

The feminists were the first to mount an active revolt against the burden of assumed emotions that was contained in the feminine ideal and the "ideology of mother." Unequivocally they stated that the portrait of the idealized woman was a fraud initiated and cherished by men. To portray women as innocent, dependent, good and selfless, in other words, was to adhere to a standard which "had always fitted masculine wishes better than it had the facts." According to Professor Kennedy women's tacit acquiescence in this myth not only caused them to doubt themselves when unable to live up to the ideal, but insulated them from passion and erotic desire by denying them the right to think of themselves as fully sexual. Indeed, both the feminists and American moralists agreed that it was male sexual ambivalence, embodied in the notorious "double standard," which had brought about a crisis in male-female relationships. A redefinition of woman's role was needed, argued the reformers, in order to save women from the pathological effects of sheltered domesticity and, at the same time, to head off a moral breakdown within the nation. Actually, the idea of woman's victimization was employed by both sides to justify their position. The opponents of woman's equality explained that women needed to be sheltered from the sinister forces of public life, and Freudian psychology argued that women were victims of their own psychic natures. On the other hand, the advocates of woman's rights argued that female Americans required the ballot, as well as legal, economic and social reforms in their status, for self-protection.

* For a discussion of the New Woman's particular predicament see "Woman As Alien," Christopher Lasch, *The New Radicalism in America: 1889–1963: The Intellectual As A Social Type* (New York, 1965), pp. 38–68.

In the late nineteenth century . . . the age-old discussion of woman's place was just beginning to take on its modern urgency. No longer could that discussion be academic, as it had been earlier in the century: the New Woman was appearing on the scene and demanding to be taken seriously. The New Woman was in fact two different ladies, the self-sufficient working girl and the dependent, restless "parasite woman," the idle wife in a middle class with growing wealth and leisure. But each of these women was new, and each, in her own way, repudiated the nineteenth-century ideal of femininity. . . .

. . . The nineteenth-century woman, said Mary Roberts Coolidge, a perceptive and sympathetic critic of the feminist movement, was raised to please men, not herself. Woman's personality had come to resemble that of an actor, who, "like the woman," Mrs. Coolidge wrote, "makes his place in life chiefly by the cultivation of manner and appearance. He, like her, depends for success upon pleasing rather than being admirable. The 'matinee idol' is an extreme example of character—or, rather, perversion of character—by the social necessity of being charming and of trading in assumed emotions."[1] Though "other-direction" has been called a characteristically twentieth-century component of personality, American women obviously knew its meaning well before 1900. So too, it could be argued, the "individualism" so highly valued in the nineteenth century and ever since regarded as a distinctive quality of American life in that epoch, was apparently for men only.

By the end of the century, however, feminists had mounted an active revolt against the burden of assumed emotions. The picture of the idealized woman, they said, was false; and certainly that picture of American women—as innocent, dependent, good, and selfless—had always fitted masculine wishes better than it had the facts.

What men cherished as "innocence" was purchased at the price of often disastrous ignorance. Charlotte Perkins Gilman indicted the belief that innocence was a woman's chief charm. "What good does it do her?" she asked. "Her whole life's success is made to depend on her marrying; her health and happiness depends [sic] on her marrying the right man. The more 'innocent' she is, the less she knows, the easier it is for the wrong man to get her." Mary Roberts

[1] Mary Roberts Coolidge, *Why Women Are So* (New York, 1912), p. 101.

Coolidge noted ironically that though marriage and motherhood constituted a woman's only permitted career, "yet, nothing in her training had any direct relation to it, and the conventional standard of modesty required her to be wholly ignorant of its physical aspects." Certainly Susan B. Anthony learned little about the "physical aspects" of married life from a mother who took her confinement literally. An anonymous feminist in 1906 said that the average nineteenth-century girl "contemplated the sexual relation with the bitterest reluctance," because she had been "sedulously guarded from knowledge of the fundamental reasons of her being, cast suddenly and unprepared into marriage." Robert Latou Dickinson, probably America's most prominent gynecologist, corroborated those women's observations when he reported that his clinical practice had shown that "no single cause of mental strain in married women is as widespread as sex fears and maladjustments." He blamed the prevalence of those fears on the enforced sexual ignorance of women.[2]

The pathologic effects of the regimen of sheltered domesticity were not all psychological. The helplessness of the American woman —especially in the urban East and the upper-class South—owed at least as much to real physiological weakness as it did to compliance with a rigid moral ideal. "An American sculptor unhampered by the models of the past," said a woman writer in 1873, "would represent the Three Graces as lolling on sofa-cushions, with a bottle of salts in one hand and a fan in the other." To be ladylike, she said, was to be "lifeless, inane, and dawdling," and another woman later recalled a nineteenth-century rhyme which told that "the bride, *of course,* fainted, for, being acquainted with manners, she knew what was right." Robert Latou Dickinson insisted in the 1890s that the neurasthenic female was more than a caricature and that the causes of her condition were plain: lack of exercise and ridiculous standards of dress. "It is supposed to be sufficient exercise for the sister," he wrote, "to wave her handkerchief from the grand stand." Dickinson also suggested that the alleged "sexlessness" of American women owed at least in part to the relatively primitive state of gynecological

[2] Charlotte Perkins Gilman, *Man-Made World* (London, 1911), p. 167; Coolidge, pp. 44–45; Elizabeth B. Wetmore, *The Secret Life* (New York, 1906), p. 93; Robert Latou Dickinson, "Marital Maladjustment—The Business of Preventive Gynecology," *Long Island Medical Journal* 2 (1908): 1–5.

medicine. Low-grade vaginal infections, later remedied routinely, could in the nineteenth century be an enduring and debilitating discomfort. And scores of other medical writers joined Dickinson in pointing out the harmful effects of the steel-ribbed corsets women wore to shrink their waists and expand their busts. The rigid "health waists" were especially damaging to working girls who leaned forward all day over a typewriter or a sewing machine. Still, in spite of almost daily evidence of the injury done to women by overdomestication and overdressing, the American male—whose house women kept and for whose eye they attired themselves—continued to pride himself on the manly protection he offered his delicate, dependent charges.[3] . . .

Finally, the myth of the idealized American woman preserved her innocence and her goodness by denying her sexuality. In nineteenth-century fiction, said Thomas Beer, "the female principal is risen above romance and becomes an opalescent cloud, dripping odors which had nothing to do with the process of childbearing at all." The myth, therefore, not only kept women ignorant of what it simultaneously glorified as their chief honor and duty. It also insulated them from all passion and erotic desire. As Viola Klein has observed, in the whole Western world "during the nineteenth and at the beginning of the twentieth century it would have been not only scandalous to admit the existence of a strong sex urge in women, but it would have been contrary to all observation." H. L. Mencken called it a "good old sub-Potomac" idea that a woman "who loses her virtue is, *ipso facto,* a victim and not a criminal or *particeps criminis,* and that a 'lady,' by virtue of being a 'lady,' is necessarily a reluctant and helpless quarry in the hunt of love." But the idea held with nearly unassailable force above the Potomac as well. No genuinely passionate woman appeared in American fiction at least from the time of the Civil War to the naturalist outburst at the turn of the century. As late as 1908, Robert Latou Dickinson was urging the medical profession to tell nervous women patients there was no cause for alarm if they enjoyed sexual intercourse. And even such an other-

[3] Mrs. Abba Woolson, *Woman in American Society* (Boston, 1873), p. 192; Margaret Deland, "Change in the Feminine Ideal," *Atlantic,* March 1910, p. 293; R. L. Dickinson, "Simple and Practical Methods in Dress Reform," *Gynecological Transactions* 18 (1893): 411; R. L. Dickinson, "Bicycling for Women from the Standpoint of the Gynecologist," *American Journal of Obstetrics* 31 (1895): 25.

wise perceptive man as E. A. Ross asserted confidently in 1906 that it was a "physiological fact that the sexual instinct is not only very much weaker in most women, but is altogether absent in a growing number of them."[4]

Feminists reacted against both the myth and the facts it so sanctimoniously concealed but could not change. By the end of the nineteenth century women were telling men that they wanted neither innocence nor ignorance, dependence nor disease, self-abnegation nor sacrifice, goodness nor sexlessness. The New Woman, Leslie Fiedler has said, refused to accept her prescribed function of "redemptive suffering," and with that refusal she "threatened to upset the whole Sentimental Love Religion" in which the myth of the ideal woman was enshrined. Independence became the religion of the New Woman, and Henrik Ibsen was one of its chief prophets. Ibsen showed, said one of his American admirers in 1890, "the necessity of a new life . . . a life divested of the conventional ideas of what is Woman's duty." In contrast to early feminist reformers who had sought to restructure legal forms in order to give women control over their own property and persons, by the late nineteenth century feminists more or less consciously sought to restructure the feminine personality itself.[5]

Lydia Commander, describing the New Woman in 1907, noted the "radical alteration in her personality. Under the old regime," she said, "humility, self-sacrifice, and obedience were assiduously cultivated as the highest of womanly virtues." But now, she concluded, "self-sacrifice . . . is no longer in favor. Self-development is rapidly taking its place." For many American feminists in the last quarter of the century, an encounter with European ideas—in Ibsen, Friedrich Nietzsche, Henri Bergson, or George Bernard Shaw—finally broke the long-standing tension of trying to live up to the duties of

[4] Thomas Beer, *The Mauve Decade* (Garden City, N.Y., 1926), p. 54; Viola Klein, *The Feminine Character* (New York, 1949), p. 85; H. L. Mencken, *Philosophy of Friedrich Nietzsche* (Boston, 1908), p. 186; R. L. Dickinson, "Marital Maladjustment"; E. A. Ross, "Western Civilization and the Birth Rate," American Sociological Society, *Papers and Proceedings* 1 (1907): 29–54. See Steven Marcus, *The Other Victorians: A Study of Sexuality and Pornography in Mid-Nineteenth Century England* (New York, 1966), pp. 28–32, for a most interesting discussion of a similar desexualizing of women in nineteenth-century England.
[5] Leslie Fiedler, *Love and Death in the American Novel* (New York, 1960), p. 221; Annie Nathan Meyer, letter to the editor, *Critic,* March 22, 1890, p. 148.

the feminine ideal. After more than two generations of strictly legal progress, the women's movement began to turn inward to search for a definition of a new feminine personality. Later, the movement would again turn at least partly outward and justify itself with claims of the benefits it could bestow on society. But for a season its paramount concern was the development of a new sense of self. And in that development, society, and society's expectations, could only be enemies.[6]

But though the New Woman was not to be so easily compensated, she herself nevertheless appealed to society's sense of her victimization when she did demand compensation in the shape of legal, economic, and social reforms. When the suffragists first shifted from a "natural rights" to an "expediency" argument for the vote, says Aileen Kraditor, they insisted "that women needed the ballot for self-protection." In other words, they asked for political power to combat the forces that victimized them. Similarly, protective labor legislation first came into being "in the name of defenseless women and children." And Christopher Lasch has noted perceptively that "it was not the image of women as equals that inspired the reform of the divorce laws, but the image of women as victims." In her search for equality, says Lasch, by appealing to the idea of victimization, "woman depended on a sentimentalization of womanhood which eroded the idea of equality as easily as it promoted it."[7]

Both feminists and antifeminists spoke of woman's victimization in terms of her sex. As Aileen Kraditor notes, "the antis regarded each woman's vocation as determined not by her individual capacities or wishes but by her sex. Men were expected to have a variety of ambitions and capabilities, but all women were destined from birth to be fulltime wives and mothers. To dispute this eternal truth was to challenge theology, biology, or sociology."[8] Feminists flirted occasionally with the idea that their distinctive sexual characteristics made them superior. That idea proceeded logically from the feminine myth which told women they were purer, more generous, and morally better than men. But more often women, in their quest for a new

---

[6] Lydia Commander, *American Idea* (New York, 1907), pp. 144–145.
[7] Aileen Kraditor, *The Idea of the Woman Suffrage Movement, 1890–1920* (New York, 1965), p. 54; Christopher Lasch, "Divorce and the Family," *Atlantic*, November, 1966, p. 59.
[8] Kraditor, p. 15.

definition of self, resented what Elsie Clews Parsons, a prominent woman sociologist, called "the domination of personality by sex." When the feminists talked about sex, they did not intend the word as it is usually understood today. Today, "sex" has an erotic meaning. It generally connotes instinct, passion, emotion, stimulation, pleasure, often intercourse itself. But the nineteenth-century feminists used "sex" almost exclusively to denote gender. For them, "sex" indicated all the special feminine characteristics men used to differentiate and, said the feminists, to subjugate women. Charlotte Perkins Gilman repeatedly condemned what she called masculine oversexualization of the world; she was speaking not of pornography or lechery but of a caste system which kept women in their place. Men saw "nothing in the world *but* sex, either male or female," she argued, and in such an atmosphere neither men nor women could develop the truly human qualities common to each. "Our distinctions of sex," she said, "are carried to such a degree as to be disadvantageous to our progress as individuals and as a race." For women like Mrs. Gilman and Mrs. Parsons, the new feminine personality could only emerge when sex became "a factor, not an obsession." Then "relations between men and women will be primarily personal relations, secondarily sexual." That was the dominant feminist position, though some other feminist sympathizers, such as Ellen Key, and even, in his own way, Theodore Roosevelt, promoted the alternative view that women had a separate sexual identity but were nevertheless the equals of men. In any case, all the theories about the relation of feminine sex characteristics to personality manifested a conscious effort to define, or to redefine, woman's role.[9] . . .

The redefinition of woman's role encountered entrenched but confused opposition. Antifeminists argued on the one hand that woman's God-given, natural role was so immutable that the suggestion of change was ludicrous, and on the other that her sacred maternal and connubial functions were so susceptible to corruption that she must be protected from the forces of change. But the antifeminists' confusion did not temper the strenuousness of their objections. Indeed, the strength of the objections indicated anxieties that

[9] Elsie Clews Parsons, *Social Freedom* (New York, 1915), pp. 29, 36; Gilman, *Man-Made World,* p. 154; Charlotte Perkins Gilman, *Women and Economics* (New York, 1966; first published, 1898), p. 33.

only indirectly touched the question of economic and educational equality for women. Those anxieties primarily concerned the male's own social role and his sexual identity. . . .

Just as women were sentimentally venerated partly as compensation for their victimization, men, the *Nation* implied, were granted all the prerogatives of the patriarchal family to compensate for the difficulty with which they held their sexual instinct in check. In both cases, the denial of sexuality, in its modern sense of instinct, was closely tied to the nineteenth-century idea of sexual role. And in both cases, for themselves and for women, men defined the proper roles. Men saw themselves as patriarchal and authoritarian because they suppressed a sexual nature that was aggressive, even potentially brutal. And they saw woman as innocent, dependent, good, and generous because she was—ideally—sexless.

By the end of the nineteenth century, it was becoming increasingly difficult to contain real women within the myth of the feminine ideal. The emergence of the New Woman necessitated adjustments in man's role, and, less demonstrably but no less importantly, in his sexuality. Women entered the work force by the hundreds of thousands. Men showed their sensitivity to role when, often without economic logic, they allowed many newly emerging forms of employment to become exclusively women's. While women felt free to attempt almost any traditionally male job, men usually abandoned any occupation that became identified with women. G. Stanley Hall, the psychologist who brought Freud to Clark University, touched on that phenomenon in 1906 when he reported that several "independent statistical studies" showed that girls often held masculine "ideals," but that "boys almost never choose feminine ideals." In the transvaluation of sexual roles, the movement seemed to be all in one direction. Women took on traditionally masculine functions with apparently little stress; men, by contrast, feared the impairment of the very masculinity they had previously characterized as nearly beyond restraint. The "feminization" of education, Hall complained, rather than producing a desirable refinement in boys, instead unnaturally stifled their most virile traits—their "brutish elements." The fault with the women's movement, said Hall, lay in its exaggerated notion of sexual equality. The time had come, he insisted, for a "new movement . . . based upon sexual differences, not identities." He urged that course—which was in fact reactionary—not, as conservatives had previously done, for the sake of preserving a delicate femininity, but in defense of a beleaguered masculinity.[10]

Steven Marcus found in investigating the sex life of Victorian England that masculine fear of sexuality was ambivalent—men feared both impotence and potency, impulse and loss, attraction and repulsion. So too in America; ambivalence was built in. . . .

Male sexual ambivalence had underlain the notorious "double standard" against which femininists and moralists railed. "As a result of this double standard," said Dr. Prince Morrow, "society practically separates its women into two classes: from the one it demands chastity, the other is set apart for the gratification of the sexual caprices of its men. It thus proclaims the doctrine, immoral as it is unhygienic, that debauchery is a necessity for its men."[11] In either case, men made objects of women. Both the Fair Maiden and the Dark Lady served men's needs—one the needs of his conscience, the other the needs of his body. But the New Woman who came to self-consciousness toward the end of the century was no longer content to serve as a mere object. In a few years the double standard, and with it the traditional nineteenth-century idea of masculine sexuality, was under severe attack. . . .

The new notion of morality shared the endemic contempt for formalism characteristic of the early twentieth century. The old morality, as exemplified by Theodore Roosevelt, had been founded on the concept of duty; and as Roosevelt said, "The doing of duty generally means pain, hardship, self-mastery, self-denial."[12] But as the emotions grew less fearsome, they no longer needed to be so strenuously mastered and denied. As a sociologist said in 1908, "Virtue no longer consists in literal obedience to arbitrary standards set by community or church but rather in conduct consistent with the demands of a growing personality." The new morality no less than the old sprang from a sense of inwardness common to the Puritans, the proper Victorians, and the romantics; but the romantic appraisal of the inner self was by far the most sanguine. . . . And in its emphasis on the liberation of the individual personality, the new morality legitimized subjectiveness. Just as the family grew more and more

---

[10] G. Stanley Hall, "The Question of Co-Education," *Munsey's Magazine,* February 1906, pp. 588–592.

[11] Dr. Prince A. Morrow, *Social Diseases and Marriage* (New York, 1904), p. 342.

[12] Elting E. Morison (ed.), *Letters of Theodore Roosevelt,* 8 vols. (Cambridge, Mass., 1951–1954), Vol. 3, p. 521 (Roosevelt to Hamlin Garland, July 19, 1903).

private as it became increasingly an emotional center, so too did the new approval of emotionalism and subjectivism in the life of the individual reinforce the view that his conduct was his private concern. . . .

Unquestionably, Freud did much to further the liberation of sexual behavior, but in many ways Freud's influence was reactionary. For the old belief that woman was victimized by biology or by selfish men, Freud substituted the view that penis envy and a peculiar Oedipal situation made women the victims of their own psychic natures. The maternal impulse, according to the Freudians, proceeded not so much from biological and evolutionary laws as from inner psychological needs. That new thesis was scarcely less deterministic than the old. Thus Freud furnished scientific support for the old Victorian view that Nature victimized women and that they should seek compensation in wifehood and maternity. Moreover, just as sympathy was beginning at last to inform sexual relationships, Freud reemphasized sexual differences and reinstated, in a new form, the old notion of necessary sexual inequality. For Freud, the essence of masculinity was action; of femininity, passiveness. The only currency of sexual interaction, therefore, must consist of power and domination. Finally, Freud's insistence that the primary component of the emotional life was sexual, irrational, and morally uncommitted both undermined the romantic confidence in the goodness of the emotions and made them seem more important than ever. Freud diverted a romantic revolution, or emotional revolution, at its very beginning and made it a sexual revolution. The sexual revolution, though carried forward under the banner of Freudian science, would continue to show its romantic beginnings. And the women's movement, with which the revolution, by whatever name, was intimately bound up, found in Freud a false liberation. Freudian ideas proved a diversion and an obstacle which women have not yet overcome.[13] . . .

With regard to women, the new Freudian ideas shifted the sense of woman's vctimization to a different plane, but they reinforced that sense nevertheless. Just at the moment when feminists had nearly triumphed over the nineteenth-century notion of women's biological inferiority, Freud supplied a biopsychological definition of feminine inferiority which was even more difficult to combat. . . .

[13] See R. V. Sampson, *Equality and Power* (London, 1965); and Hendrik M. Ruitenbeek, *Freud and America* (New York, 1966) for the influence of Freudian ideas.

James R. McGovern

THE AMERICAN WOMAN'S PRE-WORLD WAR I FREEDOM IN MANNERS AND MORALS

The emergence of the New Woman associated with the dawning of twentieth-century American life is generally synonymous with the appearance of the "flapper" of the twenties who popularly epitomized greater freedom among women in manners and morals. Actually, according to James R. McGovern of the University of West Florida, the revolution in female behavior predates the 1920s and can be traced back to social changes that occurred in the Progressive era. Particularly after 1910, women were more "sexually emancipated" than before, and openly questioned the nineteenth-century concept of the feminine ideal. As McGovern notes, many women sloughed off numerous undergarments and loosened others in order to symbolize their "self-reliant morals" as well as to permit the ease of movement required to engage in work and recreational activities alongside of men. This mode of behavior was not restricted to younger women. Large numbers of middle-aged women as well assumed a more aggressive life-style.

Yet, as William O'Neill points out,* the liberated flapper lacked any larger social consciousness and, in the final analysis, had little understanding of "sisterhood." She was so intent upon self-satisfaction that she was unconcerned with the inequalities which women as a group experienced. The feminist admonishment to "rise up and strike another blow for freedom" was ludicrous to this type of New Woman who had personally all the freedom that she could possibly use.

A significant deterioration of external controls over morality had occurred before 1920. One of the consequences of working and living conditions in the cities, especially as these affected women, was that Americans of the period 1900–1920 had experienced a vast dissolution of moral authority, which formerly had centered in the family and the small community. The traditional "straight and narrow" could not serve the choices and opportunities of city life. As against primary controls and contacts based on face-to-face association where the norms of family, church, and small community, usually

Reprinted by permission from *The Journal of American History* (September 1968), pp. 315–33. Footnotes omitted.

* William L. O'Neill, "Feminism as a Radical Ideology," originally published in *Dissent: Explorations in the History of American Radicalism,* edited by Alfred F. Young (DeKalb, Ill., 1968), pp. 290 ff.

reinforcing each other, could be internalized, the city made for a type of "individualization" through its distant, casual, specialized, and transient clusters of secondary associations. The individual came to determine his own behavioral norms.

The "home is in peril" became a fact of sociological literature as early as 1904. One of the most serious signs of its peril was the increasing inability of parents to influence their children in the delicate areas of propriety and morals. The car, already numerous enough to affect dating and premarital patterns, the 'phone coming to be used for purposes of romantic accommodation, and the variety of partners at the office or the factory, all together assured unparalleled privacy and permissiveness between the sexes.

Individualization of members served to disrupt confidence between generations of the family, if not to threaten parents with the role of anachronistic irrelevance. Dorothy Dix observed in 1913 that there had been "so many changes in the conditions of life and point of view in the last twenty years that the parent of today is absolutely unfitted to decide the problems of life for the young man and woman of today. This is particularly the case with women because the whole economic and social position of women has been revolutionized since mother was a girl." Magazine articles lamented "The Passing of the Home Daughter" who preferred the blessed anonymity of the city to "dying of asphyxiation at home!" The same phenomenon helps to explain the popularity in this period of such standardized mothers as Dorothy Dix, Beatrice Fairfax, and Emily Post, each of whom was besieged with queries on the respective rights of mothers and daughters.

Woman's individualization resulted mainly because, whether single or married, gainfully employed or not, she spent more time outside her home. Evidence demonstrates that the so-called job and kitchen revolutions were already in advanced stages by 1910. The great leap forward in women's participation in economic life came between 1900 and 1910; the percentage of women who were employed changed only slightly from 1910 to 1930. A comparison of the percentages of gainfully employed women aged sixteen to forty-four between 1890 and 1930 shows that they comprised 21.7 percent of Americans employed in 1890, 23.5 percent in 1900, 28.1 percent in 1910, 28.3 percent in 1920, and 29.7 percent in 1930. While occupational activity for women appears to stagnate from 1910 to 1920, in reality a considerable restructuring occurred with women leaving roles as domestics and assuming positions affording more personal independence as clerks and stenographers. . . .

It was in this setting that the flapper appeared along with her older married sister who sought to imitate her. No one at the office or in the next block cared much about their morals as long as the one was efficient and the other paid her bills on time. And given the fact that both these women had more leisure and wished "to participate in what men call 'the game of life'" rather than accept "the mere humdrum of household duties," it is little wonder that contemporaries rightly assessed the danger of the situation for traditional morals by 1910.

The ensuing decade was marked by the development of a revolution in manners and morals; its chief embodiment was the flapper who was urban-based and came primarily from the middle and upper classes. Young—whether in fact or fancy—assertive, and independent, she experimented with intimate dancing, permissive favors, and casual courtships or affairs. She joined men as comrades, and the differences in behavior of the sexes were narrowed. She became in fact in some degree desexualized. She might ask herself, "Am I Not a Boy? Yes, I Am—Not." Her speech, her interest in thrills and excitement, her dress and hair, her more aggressive sexuality, even perhaps her elaborate beautification, which was a statement of intentions, all point to this. Women, whether single or married, became at once more attractive and freer in their morals and paradoxically less feminine. Indeed, the term sexual revolution as applied to the Progressive era means reversal in the traditional role of women just at it describes a pronounced familiarity of the sexes.

The unmarried woman after 1910 was living in the "Day of the Girl." Dorothy Dix described "the type of girl that the modern young man falls for" in 1915 as a "husky young woman who can play golf all day and dance all night, and drive a motor car, and give first aid to the injured if anybody gets hurt, and who is in no more danger of swooning than he is." Little wonder she was celebrated in song as "A Dangerous Girl"; the lyrics of one of the popular songs for 1916 read, "You dare me, you scare me, and still I like you more each day. But you're the kind that will charm; and then do harm; you've got a dangerous way." The "most popular art print . . . ever issued" by *Puck* depicts a made-up young lady puckering her lips

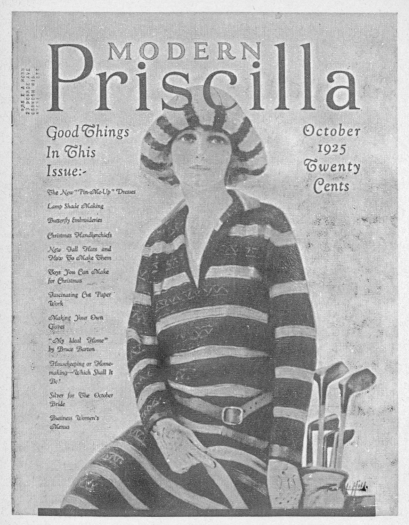

FIGURE 7. The "liberated" flapper of the late teens and twenties, while ascribing to new fashions and activities, stopped short of a serious reevaluation of womanhood.

and saying "Take It From Me!" The American girl of 1900 was not described in similar terms. The lovely and gracious Gibson Girl was too idealized to be real. And when young lovers trysted in advertising, they met at Horlick's Malted Milk Bar; he with his guitar, and she with her parasol. Beatrice Fairfax could still reply archaically about the need for "maidenly reserve" to such queries as those on the proprieties of men staring at women on the streets. And the *Wellesley College News* in 1902 reported that students were not permitted to have a Junior Prom because it would be an occasion for meeting "promiscuous men," although the college sanctioned "girl dances."

The girls, however, dispensed with "maidenly reserve." In 1910, Margaret Deland, the novelist, could announce a "Change in the Feminine Ideal."

> *This young person . . . with surprisingly bad manners—has gone to college, and when she graduates she is going to earn her own living . . . she won't go to church; she has views upon marriage and the birth-rate, and she utters them calmly, while her mother blushes with embarrassment; she occupies herself, passionately, with everything except the things that used to occupy the minds of girls.*

Many young women carried their own latchkeys. Meanwhile, as Dorothy Dix noted, it had become "literally true that the average father does not know, by name or sight, the young man who visits his daughter and who takes her out to places of amusement." She was distressed over the widespread use by young people of the car which she called the "devil's wagon." Another writer asked: "Where Is Your Daughter This Afternoon?" "Are you sure that she is not being drawn into the whirling vortex of afternoon 'trots' . . . ?" Polly, Cliff Sterrett's remarkable comic-strip, modern girl from *Polly and Her Pals,* washed dishes under the shower and dried them with an electric fan; and while her mother tried hard to domesticate her, Polly wondered, "Gee Whiz! I wish I knew what made my nose shine!"

Since young women were working side by side with men and recreating more freely and intimately with them, it was inevitable that they behave like men. Older people sometimes carped that growing familiarity meant that romance was dead or that "nowadays brides hardly blush, much less faint." And Beatrice Fairfax asked, "Has Sweet Sixteen Vanished?" But some observers were encouraged to note that as girls' ways approximated men's, the sexes were, at least, more comradely. The modern unmarried woman had become a "Diana, Hunting in the Open." Dorothy Dix reported that "nice girls, good girls, girls in good positions in society—frankly take the initiative in furthering an acquaintance with any man who happens to strike their fancy." The new ideal in feminine figure, dress, and hair styles was all semi-masculine. The "1914 Girl" with her "slim hips and boy-carriage" was a "slim, boylike creature." The "new figure is Amazonian, rather than Miloan. It is boyish rather than womanly. It is strong rather than soft." Her dress styles, meanwhile, deemphasized both hips and bust while they permitted the large waist. The boyish coiffure began in 1912 when young women began to tuck-under their hair with a ribbon; and by 1913–1914, Newport ladies, actresses like Pauline Frederick, then said to be the prettiest girl in America, and the willowy, popular dancer Irene Castle were wearing short hair. By 1915, the *Ladies Home Journal* featured women with short hair on its covers, and even the pure type of woman who advertised Ivory Soap appeared to be shorn.

The unmarried flapper was a determined pleasure-seeker whom novelist Owen Johnson described collectively as "determined to liberate their lives and claim the same rights of judgment as their brothers." The product of a "feminine revolution startling in the shock of its abruptness," she was living in the city independently of her family. Johnson noted: "She is sure of one life only and that one she passionately desires. She wants to live that life to its fullest. . . . She wants adventure. She wants excitement and mystery. She wants to see, to know, to experience. . . ." She expressed both a "passionate revolt against the commonplace" and a "scorn of conventions." Johnson's heroine in *The Salamander,* Doré Baxter, embodied his views. Her carefree motto is reminiscent of Fitzgerald's flappers of the Twenties: " 'How do I know what I'll do tomorrow?' " Her nightly prayer, the modest " 'O Lord! give me everything I want!' " Love was her "supreme law of conduct," and she, like the literary flappers of the twenties, feared "thirty as a sort of sepulcher, an end of all things!" Johnson believed that all young women in all sections of the country had "a little touch of the Salamander," each alike being impelled by "an impetuous frenzy . . . to sample each new excitement," both the "safe and the dangerous." Girls "seemed determined to have their fling like men," the novelist Gertrude Atherton noted in *Current Opinion,* "and some of the stories [about them] made even my sophisticated hair crackle at the roots. . . ." Beatrice Fairfax deplored the trends, especially the fact that "Making love lightly, boldly and promiscuously seems to be part of our social structure." Young men and women kissed though they did not intend to marry. And kissing was shading into spooning (" 'To Spoon' or 'Not to Spoon' Seems to Be the Burning Question with Modern Young America") and even petting," which was modish among the collegiate set. In fact, excerpts from the diary of a coed written before World War I suggest that experimentation was virtually complete within her peer group. She discussed her "adventures" with other college girls. "We were healthy animals and we were demanding our rights to spring's awakening." As for men, she wrote, "I played square with the men. I always told them I was not out to pin them down to marriage, but that this intimacy was pleasant and I wanted it as much as they did. We indulged in sex talk, birth control. . . . We thought too much about it."

One of the most interesting developments in changing sexual behavior which characterized these years was the blurring of age lines between young and middle-aged women in silhouette, dress, and cosmetics. A fashion commentator warned matrons, "This is the day of the figure. . . . The face alone, no matter how pretty, counts for nothing unless the body is as straight and yielding as every young girl's." With only slight variations, the optimum style for women's dress between 1908 and 1918 was a modified sheath, straight up and down and clinging. How different from the styles of the high-busted, broad-hipped mother of the race of 1904 for whom Ella Wheeler Wilcox, the journalist and poet, advised the use of veils because "the slightest approach to masculinity in woman's attire is always unlovely and disappointing."

The sloughing off of numerous undergarments and loosening of others underscored women's quickening activity and increasingly self-reliant morals. Clinging dresses and their "accompanying lack of undergarments" eliminated, according to the president of the New York Cotton Exchange, "at least twelve yards of finished goods for each adult female inhabitant." Corset makers were forced to make adjustments too and use more supple materials. Nevertheless, their sales declined. . . .

In her dress as well as her use of cosmetics, the American woman gave evidence that she had abandoned passivity. An unprecedented public display of the female figure characterized the period. Limbs now became legs and more of them showed after 1910, although they were less revealing than the promising hosiery advertisements.

Rolled down hose first appeared in 1917. Dresses for opera and restaurant were deeply cut in front and back, and not even the rumor that Mrs. John Jacob Astor had suffered a chest cold as a result of wearing deep decolleté deterred their wearers. As for gowns, "Fashion says—Evening gowns must be sleeveless . . . afternoon gowns are made with semi-transparent yokes and sleeves." Undoubtedly, this vogue for transparent blouses and dresses caused the editor of the *Unpopular Review* to declare: "At no time and place under Christianity, except the most corrupt periods in France . . . certainly never before in America, has woman's form been so freely displayed in society and on the street."

In addition to following the example of young women in dress and beautification, middle-aged women, especially those from the middle and upper classes, were espousing their permissive manners and morals. Smoking and, to a lesser extent, drinking in public were becoming fashionable for married women of the upper class and were making headway at other class levels. As early as 1910, a prominent clubwoman stated: "It has become a well-established habit for women to drink cocktails. It is thought the smart thing to do." . . . They conscientiously practiced birth control, as did women of other classes. And they initiated divorce proceedings, secure in the knowledge that many of their best friends had done the same thing. . . .

Insights regarding the attitudies of married women from the urban lower middle class can be found in the diary of Ruth Vail Randall, who lived in Chicago from 1911 to the date of her suicide, March 6, 1920. A document of urban sociology, the diary transcends mere personal experience and becomes a commentary on group behavior of the times. Mrs. Randall was reared in a family that owned a grocery store, was graduated from high school in Chicago, and was married at twenty to Norman B. Randall, then twenty-one. She worked after marriage in a department store and later for a brief period as a model. She looked to marriage, especially its romance, as the supreme fulfillment of her life and was bitterly disappointed with her husband. She began to turn to other men whom she met at work or places of recreation, and her husband left her. Fearing that her lover would leave her eventually as well, she killed him and herself.

The diary focuses on those conditions which made the revolution in morals a reality. The young couple lived anonymously in a highly mobile neighborhood where their morals were of their own making. Mrs. Randall did not want children; she aborted their only child. She was also averse to the reserved "womanly" role, which her husband insisted that she assume. She complained, "Why cannot a woman do all man does?" She wished that men and women were more alike in their social roles. She repudiated involvement in her home, resolved to exploit equally every privilege which her husband assumed, drank, flirted, and lived promiscuously. Telephones and cars made her extramarital liaisons possible. Even before her divorce, she found another companion; flounting convention, she wrote, "He and I have entered a marriage pact according to our own ideas." Throughout her diary she entertained enormous, almost magical, expectations of love. She complained that her lovers no more than her husband provided what she craved—tenderness and companionship. Disillusionment with one of them caused her to cry out, "I am miserable. I have the utmost contempt for myself. But the lake is near and soon it will be warm. Oh, God to rest in your arms. To rest —and to have peace." . . .

The revolution in manners and morals, particularly as it affected women, took the twofold form of more permissive sexuality and diminished femininity. Women from the upper classes participated earlier, as is evidenced by their introductory exhibition of fashions, hair styles, dances, cosmetics, smoking, and drinking. Realistic novels concerned with marriage suggest that they entertained ideas of promiscuity and even infidelity before women of the lower classes. Yet the cardinal condition of change was not sophistication but urban living and the freedom it conferred. As technology and economic progress narrowed the gap between the classes, middle-class women and even those below were free to do many of the same things almost at the same time. Above all, the revolution in manners and morals after 1910 demonstrates that sexual freedom and the twentieth-century American city go together.

Further Reading

Because Professor McGovern's essay argues for a revision of currently held views, his sources are almost exclusively primary, consisting largely of articles from magazines such as *Atlantic, Cosmopolitan* and *Ladies Home Journal.* McGovern's thesis is a corrective to the interpretation of the change in manners and morals found in Frederick L. Allen's *Only Yesterday: An Informal History of the Nineteen-Twenties* (New York, 1931); William Leuchtenburg's *The Perils of Prosperity: 1914–1932* (Chicago, 1958); and George Mowry's *The Urban Nation: 1920–1960* (New York, 1965). Read as well Kenneth Yellis' article, "Prosperity's Child: Some Thoughts on the Flapper," *American Quarterly* (Spring, 1969), pp. 44–64.

Alice S. Rossi

EQUALITY BETWEEN THE SEXES:
AN IMMODEST PROPOSAL

This essay about the recent past quite appropriately comes from the pen of a sociologist, Alice S. Rossi (b. 1922) of Goucher College. In her 1964 work, which is already a classic in women's studies, Professor Rossi poses three basic questions: Why did feminism decline after 1920? Why is equality between the sexes desirable? And by what means can the latter be achieved? The following selection deals primarily with the second question.*

Rossi's contention is that inequality between the sexes, symbolized by the use of the traditional concepts of "masculine" and "feminine," has been detrimental to a healthy development of American society in the second half of the twentieth century. Such an understanding of sex roles is not only debilitating for women, but for men and children as well. At the heart of the matter, notes Rossi, is the preoccupation of women with motherhood as a full-time occupation. Sociologist Phillip E. Slater has referred to this post–World War II phenomenon as the "ultra-domestication of the American middle-class female." Professor Rossi, like Slater, sees the magnification of childbearing as an extension of "make-work" which is promoted and/or reinforced by "experts" such as Dr. Benjamin Spock who induce guilt in women who are not "fully committed" to motherhood. For Rossi, a well-balanced understanding of womanhood requires meaningful work outside of the home, such as a profession. In order to achieve this, she argues, the geographical separation between the suburban home and work must be reconsidered . . . for the benefit of fatherhood as well as motherhood. Otherwise, as Slater puts it, American society will continue to be divided into two cultures, one where husbands go to participate in the twentieth century and another where wives are assigned the hopeless task of trying to act out a nineteenth century bucolic fantasy.†

. . . the principle which regulates the existing relations between the two sexes . . . is wrong in itself and [is] now the chief hindrance to human

Reprinted by permission of *Daedalus,* Journal of the American Academy of Arts and Sciences, Boston, Mass., Spring 1964, *The Woman in America,* pp. 607–52. Footnotes omitted.

* For an Introduction to the first question see William L. O'Neill, "Feminism as a Radical Ideology," *Dissent: Explorations in the History of American Radicalism,* edited by Alfred F. Young (DeKalb, Ill., 1968). The third question has received prolonged attention from the revitalized feminist movement, some of which sources are cited at the end of this essay.

† It is interesting to compare Rossi's essay with Slater's, written six years later, in order to note how contemporary her observations still are: "Women and Children First, the Spockian Challenge," *The Pursuit of Loneliness: American Culture at the Breaking Point* (Boston, 1970), especially pp. 64–75.

improvement; and . . . it ought to be replaced by a principle of perfect equality, admitting no power or privilege on the one side, nor disability on the other.

John Stuart Mill, 1869

When John Stuart Mill wrote his essay on "The Subjection of Women" in 1869, the two major things he argued for with elegance and persuasion were to extend the franchise to women, and to end the legal subordination of married women to their husbands. The movement for sex equality had already gathered considerable momentum in England and the United States by 1869, reaching its peak fifty years later, when the franchise was won by American women in 1920. In the decades since 1920, this momentum has gradually slackened, until by the 1960s American society has been losing rather than gaining ground in the growth toward sex equality. . . .

It will be the major thesis of this essay that we need to reassert the claim to sex equality and to search for the means by which it can be achieved. By sex equality I mean a socially androgynous conception of the roles of men and women, in which they are equal and similar in such spheres as intellectual, artistic, political and occupational interests and participation, complementary only in those spheres dictated by physiological differences between the sexes. This assumes the traditional conceptions of masculine and feminine are inappropriate to the kind of world we can live in in the second half of the twentieth century. An androgynous conception of sex role means that each sex will cultivate some of the characteristics usually associated with the other in traditional sex-role definitions. This means that tenderness and expressiveness should be cultivated in boys and socially approved in men, so that a male of any age in our society would be psychologically and socially free to express these qualities in his social relationships. It means that achievement need, workmanship and constructive aggression should be cultivated in girls and approved in women so that a female of any age would be similarly free to express these qualities in her social relationships. This is one of the points of contrast with the feminist goal of an earlier day: rather than a one-sided plea for women to adapt a masculine stance in the world, this definition of sex equality stresses the enlargement of the common ground on which men and women base their lives together by changing the social definitions of approved characteristics and behavior for both sexes.

It will be an assumption of this essay that by far the majority of the differences between the sexes which have been noted in social research are socially rather than physiologically determined. What proportion of these sex differences are physiologically based and what proportion are socially based is a question the social and physiological sciences cannot really answer at the present time. It is sufficient for my present purposes to note that the opportunities for social change toward a closer approximation of equality between the sexes are large enough within the area of sex differences now considered to be socially determined to constitute a challenging arena for thought and social action. This is my starting point. I shall leave to speculative discourse and future physiological research the question of what constitutes irreducible differences between the sexes. . . .

. . . It is the traditional image of woman which is popularized: the woman who finds complete self-fulfillment in her exclusive devotion to marriage and parenthood. Women who thirty years ago might have chosen a career over a marriage, or restricted their family size to facilitate the combination of family and work roles, have been persuaded to believe that such choices reflect their inadequacy as women. It is this sense of failure as a woman that lies behind the defensive and apologetic note of many older unmarried professional women, the guilt which troubles the working mother (which I suspect goes up in direct proportion to the degree to which she is familiar with psychoanalytic ideas), the restriction of the level of aspiration of college women, the early plunge into marriage, the closed door of the doll's house.

Our society has been so inundated with psychoanalytic thinking that any dissatisfaction or conflict in personal and family life is considered to require solution on an individual basis. This goes well with the general American value stress on individualism, and American women have increasingly resorted to psychotherapy, the most highly individualized solution of all, for the answers to the problems they have as women. In the process the idea has been lost that many problems, even in the personal family sphere, cannot be solved on an individual basis, but require solution on a societal level by changing the institutional contexts within which we live.

The consequences of this acceptance of psychoanalytic ideas and conservatism in the social sciences have been twofold: first, the social sciences in the United States have contributed very little since the 1930s to any lively intellectual dialogue on sex equality as a goal or the ways of implementing that goal. Second, they have provided a quasi-scientific underpinning to educators, marriage counselors, mass media and advertising researchers, who together have partly created, and certainly reinforced, the withdrawal of millions of young American women from the mainstream of thought and work in our society.

. . . Why should American society attempt to reach a state of sex equality? If women seem satisfied with a more narrowly restricted life pattern than men would be, why should we seek to disturb this pattern? To begin with, I do not think this question is really relevant to the issue. There have been underprivileged groups throughout history which contained sizable proportions of contented, uncomplaining members, whether slaves, serfs or a low-status caste. But the most enlightened members of both the privileged and underprivileged groups in such societies came to see that inequality not only depressed the human potential of the subject groups but corrupted those in the superordinate groups. The lives of southern whites are as crippled by racial inequality as the lives of southern Negroes are impoverished. In the same way, many men spend their daytime hours away from home as vital cognitive animals and their nights and weekends in mental passivity and vegetation. Social and personal life is impoverished for some part of many men's lives because so many of their wives live in a perpetual state of intellectual and social impoverishment.

A second reason why American society should attempt to reach a state of full sex equality is that at the level our industrial society has now reached, it is no longer necessary for women to confine their life expectations to marriage and parenthood. Certain of the reasons for this have been increasingly stressed in recent years: with increased longevity, and smaller sized families, the traditional mother role simply does not occupy a sufficient portion of a woman's life span to constitute any longer the exclusive adult role for which a young woman should be prepared. American girls spend more time as apprentice mothers with their dolls than they will as adult women with their own babies, and there is half a lifetime still ahead by the time the youngest child enters high school. Although studies have shown that women today are working in the home roughly the same number of hours a week as their mothers did, this is not because they have to do so: technological innovations in the production and distribution of food, clothing and other household equipment have been such that homemaking no longer requires the specialized skills and time-consuming tasks it did until early in our century. Contemporary women often turn what should be labor-saving devices into labor-making devices. In the light of the many time-consuming tasks the American mother fifty years ago had to perform, and the much longer work day for those in the labor force then, the woman in 1964 who holds down a full-time job will probably have as much or more time with her children as her grandmother had. Furthermore, most of the skills needed for adulthood are no longer taught within the family: child socialization is increasingly a shared enterprise between the parent and teachers, doctors, nurses, club leaders and instructors in an assortment of special skills.

These are perhaps all familiar points. What has not been seen is the more general point that *for the first time in the history of any known society, motherhood has become a full-time occupation for adult women.* In the past, whether a woman lived on a farm, a Dutch city in the seventeenth century, or a colonial town in the eighteenth century, women in all strata of society except the very top were never able to be full-time mothers as the twentieth-century middle-class American woman has become. These women were productive members of farm and craft teams along with their farmer, baker or printer husbands and other adult kin. Children either shared in the work of the household or were left to amuse themselves; their mothers did not have the time to organize their play, worry about their development, discuss their problems. These women were not lonely because the world came into their homes in the form of customers, clients or patients in villages and towns, or farmhands and relatives on the farm; such women had no reason to complain of the boredom and solitude of spending ten-hour days alone with babies and young children because their days were peopled with adults. There were no child specialists to tell the colonial merchant's wife or pioneer farmer's wife that her absorption in spinning, planting, churning and preserving left her children on their own too much, that how she fed her baby would shape his adult personality, or that leaving children with a variety of other adults while she worked would make them insecure.

There are two important questions this analysis raises: why has full-time motherhood been accepted by the overwhelming majority of American women, and how successful has been the new pattern of full-time motherhood of the past forty years or so? I believe the major answer to the first question is that the American woman has been encouraged by the experts to whom she has turned for guidance in child-rearing to believe that her children need her continuous presence, supervision and care and that she should find complete fulfillment in this role. If, for example, a woman reads an article by Dr. Spock on working mothers, she is informed that any woman who finds full-time motherhood produces nervousness is showing a "residue of difficult relationships in her own childhood"; if irritability and nervousness are not assuaged by a brief trip or two, she is probably in an emotional state which can be "relieved through regular counseling in a family social agency, or, if severe, through psychiatric treatment"; and finally, "any mother of a preschool child who is considering a job should discuss the issues with a social worker before making her decision."* Since the social worker shares the same analytic framework that Dr. Spock does, there is little doubt what the advice will be; the woman is left with a judgment that wanting more than motherhood is not natural but a reflection of her individual emotional disturbance.

The fundamental tenet of the theory underlying such advice is that the physically and emotionally healthy development of the infant requires the loving involvement of the mother with the child. If an infant does not receive stable continuous mothering there is almost invariably severe physical and emotional disturbance. There is apparently ample clinical evidence to support these points. Studies have suggested that prolonged separation from parents, and particularly from the mother, has serious effects upon infants and young children. However, practitioners make unwarranted extrapolations from these findings when they advise that *any* separation of mother and child is risky and hazardous for the healthy development of the child. Despite the fact that the empirical evidence stems from instances of prolonged, traumatic separation caused by such things as

---

* Benjamin Spock, "Should Mothers Work?" *Ladies Home Journal* (February 1963).

the death or serious illness of the mother, or the institutionalization of the child, this viewpoint is applied to the situation of an employed mother absent from the home on a regular basis. No one predicts that any dire consequences will flow from a woman's absence from home several afternoons a week to engage in a shopping spree, keep medical appointments or play bridge; nor is a father considered to produce severe disturbance in his young children even if his work schedule reduces contact with them to the daylight hours of a weekend. But women who have consulted pediatricians and family counselors about their resuming work are firmly told that they should remain at home, for the sake of their children's emotional health.

What effect *does* maternal employment have upon children? Many sociologists of the family have raised this question during the past fifteen years, expecting to find negative effects as psychoanalytic theory predicted. In fact, the focus of most maternal employment studies has been on the effect of mothers' working upon the personalities of their children, somewhat less often on the tensions and strains between the mother role and the occupational role, seldom on the question of how maternal employment affects the woman's satisfactions with herself, her home and marriage. To date, *there is no evidence of any negative effects traceable to maternal employment;* children of working mothers are no more likely than children of nonworking mothers to become delinquent, to show neurotic symptoms, to feel deprived of maternal affection, to perform poorly in school, to lead narrower social lives, etc. Many of the researchers in the 1950s frankly admitted surprise at their negative findings. In a study reported in 1962, the only significant difference found between working and nonworking mothers was the mother's confidence about her role as mother: 42 percent of the working mothers but only 24 percent of the nonworking mothers expressed concern about their maternal role, "often by explicit questioning and worry as to whether working is interfering with their relationships and the rearing of their children." Yet these working women did not actually differ from the at-home mothers in the very things that concerned them: there were no differences between these women in the emotional relationships with their children, household allocation of responsibilities, principles of child-rearing, etc. The working mothers appeared to share the prevailing view that their children would suffer as a result of their employment, though in fact their children fare as well as those of nonworking mothers.

It would appear, therefore, that the employment of women when their children are eight years of age or older has no negative effect on the children. What about the earlier years, from infancy until school age? In the American literature, there is little to refer to as yet which bears directly upon the effect of maternal employment on the infant or toddler, partly because employment of mothers with preschool children is so negligible in the United States, partly because the measurement of "effects" on young children is difficult and cannot be done with the research tools which have been used in most studies of maternal employment effects—questionnaires administered to mothers and to their school-age children.

There is, however, one significant body of data which is of considerable relevance to the question of the effect of maternal employment upon infants and very young children. Maternal employment is a regular pattern of separation of mother and child: the Israeli kibbutzim are collective settlements with several decades of experience in precisely this pattern. On the kibbutz, infants live in children's houses where their physical care and training are largely handled. During the infancy months the mother visits the house to feed the infant; as toddlers, children begin a pattern of visiting with their parents for a few hours each day, living in the children's houses for the remaining portions of their days and nights. A number of studies have been conducted to investigate the effect of this intermittent multiple-mothering on the young child. They all point to essentially the same conclusion; the kibbutz child-rearing practices have no deleterious effects upon the subsequent personality development of the children involved. In fact, there are a number of respects in which the kibbutz-reared Israeli children exceed those reared in the traditional farm family: the kibbutz children showed a more accurate perception of reality, more breadth of interest and cultural background, better emotional control and greater overall maturity.

Continuous mothering, even in the first few years of life, does not seem to be necessary for the healthy emotional growth of a child. The crux of the matter appears to be in the nature of the care which is given to the child. If a child is reared by a full-time mother who is rejecting and cold in her treatment of him, or if a child is reared in an institutional setting lacking in warmth and stimulation and with an inadequate staff, both children will show personality disturbances in later years. If the loving care of the biological mother is shared by other adults who provide the child with a stable loving environment, the child will prosper at least as well as and potentially better than one with a good full-time mother. . . .

Turning now to the second question raised above: how successful has the new pattern of full-time motherhood been? Are women more satisfied with their lives in the mid-twentieth century than in the past? Does motherhood fulfill them, provide them with a sufficient canvas to occupy a lifetime? Are contemporary children living richer lives, developing greater ego strength to carry them through a complex adulthood? Are children better off for having full-time mothers?

I think the answer to all the questions posed above is a firm *no.* Educators, child psychologists and social analysts report an increasing tendency for American middle-class children to be lacking in initiative, excessively dependent on others for direction and decision, physically soft. Our children have more toys and play equipment than children in any other society, yet they still become bored and ask their mothers for "something to do." No society has as widespread a problem of juvenile delinquency and adolescent rebellion as the United States. Alcoholism, compulsive sex-seeking and adolescent delinquency are no longer social problems confined to the working-class, socially disorganized sections of our cities, but have been on the increase in the middle-class suburb in the past twenty years, and involve more women and girls than in the past. There is a strong strand of male protest against the mother or "matriarch" in both our beatnik culture and our avant-garde literature: social and artistic extremes are seldom fully deviant from the middle range in a society, but show in an exaggerated heightened way the same though less visible tendencies in the social majority.

In a large proportion of cases, the etiology of mental illness is linked to inadequacy in the mother-child relationship. A high proportion of the psychoneurotic discharges from the army during World War II was traced to these young soldiers' overly dependent relationships to their mothers. This has been the subject of much earnest discussion in the years since the war, but the focus has remained on the mother-*son* relationship, I suspect only because as a fighter, a professional man or a worker, male performance is seen to be more crucial for society than female performance. But dependence, immaturity and ego diffusion have been characteristic of daughters as well as sons. The only difference is that, in the case of daughters, this less often reaches the overt level of a social problem because young women move quickly from under their mothers' tutelage into marriage and parenthood of their own: female failures are therefore not as socially visible, for they are kept within the privacy of family life and psychoanalytic case records. It is a short-sighted view indeed to consider the immature wife, dominating mother or interfering mother-in-law as a less serious problem to the larger society than the male homosexual, psychoneurotic soldier or ineffectual worker, for it is the failure of the mother which perpetuates the cycle from one generation to the next, affecting sons and daughters alike.

Disturbing trends of this sort cannot all be traced to the American woman's excessive and exclusive involvement with home and family. We live in turbulent times, and some part of these trends reflects the impact of world tension and conflict. But there is no reason to assume that world tension is relevant to many of them. Emotional and physical difficulties after childbirth or during the menopause years, the higher incidence of college girl than college boy breakdowns, the shrunken initiative and independence of children, are clearly not explained by world conflict. Besides, vast sections of American society remain totally unmoved and unaffected by international political and military events until they directly impinge on their own daily lives. Since history is both written and produced more by men than by women, the fact that our writers are preoccupied with the relationship to the mother points to difficulties in our family system more than the course of world events.

It is a paradox of our social history that motherhood has become a full-time occupation in precisely the era when objectively it could, and perhaps should, be a part-time occupation for a short phase of a woman's life span. I suspect that the things women do for and with their children have been needlessly elaborated to make motherhood a full-time job. Unfortunately, in this very process the child's struggle for autonomy and independence, for privacy and the right to worry things through for himself are subtly and pervasively reduced by the omnipresent mother. As a young child he is given great per-

FIGURE 8. The ultra-domestication of the American housewife since World War II has been the focus for an increasing amount of social criticism in the past decade. (*Courtesy*, Ms. *Magazine*)

missive freedom, but he must exercise it under supervision. As an adolescent he is given a great deal of freedom, but his parents worry excessively about what he does with it. Edgar Friedenberg has argued that there is entirely too much parental concentration on adolescent children, with the result that it has become increasingly difficult to *be* an adolescent in American society. He suggests that parents are interested in youth to the extent that they find their own stage of life uninteresting. Middle-class children are observed and analyzed by their mothers as though they were hothouse plants psychologically, on whose personalities any pressure might leave an indelible bruise. If a woman's adult efforts are concentrated exclusively on her children, she is likely more to stifle than broaden her children's perspective and preparation for adult life. Any stress or failure in a child becomes a failure of herself, and she is therefore least likely to truly help her child precisely when the child most needs support. In myriad ways the mother binds the child to her, dampening his initiative, resenting his growing independence in adolescence, creating a subtle dependence which makes it difficult for the child to achieve full adult stature without a rebellion which leaves him with a mixture of resentment and guilt that torments him in his mother's declining years.

It seems to me no one has linked these things together adequately. Psychiatric counselors of college students frequently have as their chief task that of helping their young patients to free themselves from the entangling web of dependence upon their parents, primarily their mothers, and encouraging them to form stable independent lives of their own. In other words, if the patient is eighteen years old the analyst tries to help her free herself from her mother, but if the next patient is twenty-five years old with young children at home, the analyst tells her the children would suffer emotional damage if she left them on a regular basis to hold down a job. The very things which would reduce the excessive dependency of children before it becomes a critical problem are discouraged by the counselor or analyst during the years when the dependency is being formed. If it is true that the adult is what the child was, and if we wish adults to be assertive, independent, responsible people, then they should be reared in a way which prevents excessive dependence on a parent. They should be cared for by a number of adults in their childhood, and their parents should truly encourage their independence and responsibility during their youthful years, not merely give lip service to these parental goals. The best way to encourage such independence and responsibility in the child is for the mother to be a living model of these qualities herself. If she had an independent life of her own, she would find her stage of life interesting, and therefore be less likely to live for and through her children. By maintaining such an independent life, the American mother might finally provide her children with something she can seldom give when she is at home—a healthy dose of inattention, and a chance for adolescence to be a period of fruitful immaturity and growth. If enough American women developed vital and enduring interests outside the family and remained actively in them throughout the child-bearing years, we might then find a reduction in extreme adolescent rebellion, immature early marriages, maternal domination of children, and interference by mothers and mothers-in-law in the lives of married children.

There remains one further general characteristic of our industrial society which has relevance to the question of why American society should achieve full sex equality. Our family unit is small, for the most part geographically if not socially isolated from its kin. This small family unit is possible because of the increased longevity in highly industrialized societies. In agricultural societies, with their high rate of mortality, many parents die before they have completed the rearing of their young. The extended family provided substitutes for such parents without disturbing the basic lines of kin affiliation and property rights of these children. In our modern family system it is an unusual event for women or men to be widowed while they have young dependent children. This also means, however, that American families must fend for themselves in the many emergencies less critical than the death of a spouse: army service, long business or professional trips, prolonged physical or emotional illness, separation or divorce often require that one spouse carry the primary responsibility for the family, even if this is cushioned or supplemented by insurance, government aid, paid helpers or relatives. The insurance advertisements which show fathers bending over a cradle and begin "what would happen if?" evoke a twinge of fear in their readers precisely because parents recognize the lonely responsible positions they would be in if serious illness or death were to strike their home. In our family system, then, it is a decided asset if men and women can quickly and easily substitute for or supplement each other as parents and as breadwinners. I believe these are important elements in the structure of our economy and family system which exert pressure toward an equality between men and women. It is not merely that a companionate or equalitarian marriage is a desirable relationship between wife and husband, but that the functioning of an urban industrial society is facilitated by equality between men and women in work, marriage and parenthood.

The conclusions I have drawn from this analysis are as follows: full-time motherhood is neither sufficiently absorbing to the woman nor beneficial to the child to justify a contemporary woman's devoting fifteen or more years to it as her exclusive occupation. Sooner or later—and I think it should be sooner—women have to face the question of who they are besides their children's mother. . . .

The preferred residential pattern of the American middle class in the postwar decades has been suburban. In many sections of the country it is difficult to tell where one municipality ends and another begins, for the farm, forest and waste land between towns and cities have been built up with one housing development after another. The American family portrayed in the mass media typically occupies a house in this sprawling suburbia, and here too, are the American women, and sometimes men, whose problems are aired and analyzed with such frequency. We know a good deal about the characteristics and quality of social life in the American suburb and the problems of the men and women who live in them. We hear about the changing political complexion of the American suburbs, the struggle of residents to provide sufficient community facilities to meet their growing needs. But the social and personal difficulties of suburban women are more likely to be attributed to their early family relationships or to the contradictory nature of the socialization of girls in our society than to any characteristic of the environment in which they now live. My focus will be somewhat different: I shall examine the suburban residence pattern for the limitations it imposes on the utilization of women's creative work abilities and the participation of men in family life. Both limitations have important implications for the lives of boys and girls growing up in the suburban home.

The geographic distance between home and work has a number of implications for the role of the father-husband in the family. It reduces the hours of possible contact between children and their fathers. The hour or more men spend in cars, buses or trains may serve a useful decompression function by providing time in which to sort out and assess the experiences at home and the events of the work day, but it is questionable whether this outweighs the disadvantage of severely curtailing the early morning and late afternoon hours during which men could be with their children.

The geographic distance also imposes a rigid exclusion of the father from the events which highlight the children's lives. Commuting fathers can rarely participate in any special daytime activities at home or at school, whether a party, a play the child performs in or a conference with a teacher. It is far less rewarding to a child to report to his father at night about such a party or part in a play than to have his father present at these events. If the husband-father must work late or attend an evening function in the city, he cannot sandwich in a few family hours but must remain in the city. This is the pattern which prompted Margaret Mead to characterize the American middle-class father as the "children's mother's husband," and partly why mother looms so oversized in the lives of suburban children.

Any social mixing of family-neighborhood and job associates is reduced or made quite formal: a work colleague cannot drop in for an after-work drink or a Saturday brunch when an hour or more separates the two men and their families. The father-husband's office and work associates have a quality of unreality to both wife and children. All these things sharpen the differences between the lives of men and women—fewer mutual acquaintances, less sharing of the day's events, and perhaps most importantly, less simultaneous filling of their complementary parent roles. The image of parenthood to the child is mostly motherhood, a bit of fatherhood and practically no parenthood as a joint enterprise shared at the same time by father and mother. Many suburban parents, I suspect, spend more time together as verbal parents—discussing their children in the children's absence—than they do actively interacting with their children, the togetherness cult notwithstanding. For couples whose relationship in courtship and early marriage was equalitarian, the pressures are strong in the suburban setting for parenthood to be highly differentiated and skewed to an ascendant position of the mother. Women dominate the family, men the job world. . . .

And what of the girl? What image of the female role is she acquiring during her early years? In her primary group environment, she sees women largely in roles defined in terms that relate to her as a child—as mother, aunt, grandmother, baby-sitter—or in roles relating to the house—the cleaning, cooking, mending activities of mother and domestic helpers. Many mothers work outside the home, but the daughter often knows as little of that work as she does of her father's. Even if her own mother works, the reasons for such working that are given to the child are most often couched in terms of the mother or housewife role. Thus, a girl is seldom told that her mother works because she enjoys it or finds it very important to her own satisfaction in life, but because the money she earns will help pay for the house, a car, the daughter's clothes, dancing lessons or school tuition. In other words, working is something mothers sometimes have to do as mothers, not something mothers do as adult women. This is as misleading and distorted an image of the meaning of work as the father who tells his child he works "to take care of mummy and you" and neglects to mention that he also works because he finds personal satisfaction in doing so, or that he is contributing to knowledge, peace or the comfort of others in the society.

The young girl also learns that it is only in the family that women seem to have an important superordinate position. However high her father's occupational status outside the home, when he returns at night, he is likely to remove his white shirt and become a blue collar Mr. Fixit or mother's helper. The traditional woman's self-esteem would be seriously threatened if her husband were to play a role equal to her own in the lives and affections of her children or in the creative or managerial aspect of home management, precisely because her major sphere in which to acquire the sense of personal worth is her home and children. The lesson is surely not lost on her daughter, who learns that at home father does not know best, though outside the home men are the bosses over women, as she can see only too well in the nurse–doctor, secretary–boss, salesclerk–

store manager, space Jane–space John relationships that she has an opportunity to observe.

The view that the socialization of the girl is an easy one compared with the boy depends on the kind of woman one has in mind as an end-product of socialization. Only if the woman is to be the traditional wife-mother is present-day socialization of young girls adequate, for from this point of view the confinement to the kinds of feminine models noted above and the superordinate position of the mother in the family facilitate an easy identification. If a girl sees that women reign only at home or in a history book, whereas outside the home they are Girl Fridays to men, then clearly for many young girls the wife-mother role may appear the best possible goal to have. It should be noted, however, that identification has been viewed primarily as an either-or process—the child identifies either with the mother or the father—and not as a process in which there is a fusion of the two parent models such that identification involves a modeling of the self after mother in some respects, father in others. It is possible that those women who have led exciting, intellectually assertive and creative lives did not identify exclusively with their traditional mothers, but crossed the sex line and looked to their fathers as model sources for ideas and life commitments of their own. This is to suggest that an exclusively same-sex identification between parent and child is no necessary condition for either mentally healthy or creative adults.

If I am correct about the significance of the father in the childhoods of those women who later led creative adult lives, then an increased accessibility of the middle-class father to his daughters and greater sharing of his ideas and interests could help to counteract the narrow confines of the feminine models daughters have. Beyond this, young girls need exposure to female models in professional and scientific occupations and to women with drive and dedication who are playing innovative volunteer roles in community organizations; they need an encouragement to emulate them and a preparation for an equalitarian rather than a dominant role in parenthood. Only if a woman's self-esteem is rooted in an independent life outside her family as well as her roles within the home can she freely welcome her husband to share on an equal basis the most rewarding tasks involved in child-rearing and home maintenance.

Further Reading

In the last decade since Alice Rossi wrote "Equality Between the Sexes" there has been a great deal of scholarly activity in the field of women's studies. Although most of her sources are now dated and of too technical a nature to be useful to the undergraduate, some "earlier" works are still helpful, including Betty Friedan, *The Feminine Mystique* (New York, 1963); Alva Myrdal and Viola Klein, *Women's Two Roles: Home and Work* (London, 1956); and William Whyte, *The Organization Man* (New York, 1956). More recent studies about "sex roles" in American society are cited in Arlie Russell Hochschild's "A Review of Sex Role Research," *American Journal of Sociology* (January, 1973), pp. 1011–1029. The entire issue is devoted to "Changing Woman in a Changing Society" (edited by Joan Huber) and worth some attention. Also noteworthy are the August and November 1971 issues of the *Journal of Marriage and the Family* which are about "Sexism in Family Studies" (Pauline B. Bart, editor). Probably the best book of reading on "Sexual Mythology and the Liberation of Women" is *Masculine/Feminine* (New York, 1969), edited by Betty Roszak and Theodore Roszak, which includes Alice Rossi's later essay, "Sex Equality: The Beginning of Ideology," *The Humanist* (September–October, 1969). For a sane discussion of current women's liberation viewpoints consult Caroline Bird's *Born Female* (New York, 1968); and *Woman in Sexist Society: Studies in Power and Powerlessness,* edited by Vivian Gornick and Barbara K. Moran (New York, 1971).

The idea of the "two separate culture" development in American male-female relationships has received little formal attention from historians. The phenomenon of "male bonding" is in a limited way discussed by Lionel Tiger, *Men in Groups* (New York, 1969), while "sorority" is briefly analyzed by William Taylor and Christopher Lasch, "Two 'Kindred Spirits': Sorority and Family in New England, 1839–1846," *New England Quarterly* (March, 1963), pp. 23–41. William O'Neill ("Feminism as a Radical Ideology") suggests that "associationism"—the increasing popularity of women's societies and clubs after 1870—indicates a movement away from male-female relationships as a viable frame of reference for social interaction; Phillip Slater traces the further decline of heterosexual activity and a healthy understanding of the family to the present.

Suggestions for Additional Reading

As yet there is no comprehensive historiographical or bibliographical discussion of women in American history. Two of the better recent attempts to survey some of the literature are Ann D. Gordon, Mari Jo Buhle and Nancy E. Schrom, "Women in American Society: An Historical Contribution," *Radical America* (July-August, 1971), pp. 3–66; and Lois W. Banner, "On Writing Women's History," *Journal of Interdisciplinary History* (Autumn, 1971), pp. 347–358. To get a sense of the variety of primary and secondary sources available for research in the field, the reader would do well to look carefully at the reference notes and bibliographical essays included in this volume. In addition consult the bibliographies in Andrew Sinclair's *The Emancipation of the American Woman* (New York, 1965); Page Smith's *Daughters of the Promised Land* (Boston, 1970); or Gerda Lerner's *The Woman in American History* (Reading, Mass., 1971). One of the best ways of surveying what is being done currently in the area of women's studies and women's history is to consult the collection of course syllabuses published by KNOW (Pittsburgh), *Female Studies No. 1* (1970), edited by Sheila Tobias, and *Female Studies No. 2* (1971), edited by Florence Howe.

Historical scholarship dealing with the colonial period has been made accessible to students by the work of Eugenie Leonard, Sophie Drinker, and Miriam Holden, *The American Woman in Colonial and Revolutionary Times, 1565–1800: A Syllabus with Bibliography* (Philadelphia, 1962). "Must" reading (although dated) includes Mary Benson, *Women in Eighteenth-Century America: A Study of Opinion and Social Usage* (New York, 1935); Elizabeth A. Dexter, *Colonial Women of Affairs: Women in Business and the Professions in America before 1776* (Boston, 1924); and Alice M. Earle, *Colonial Dames and Goodwives* (Boston, 1895). Among the specific studies of interest to the student of colonial history are Cedric B. Cowing, "Sex and the Preaching in the Great Awakening," *American Quarterly* (Fall, 1968), pp. 624–644; Herbert Moller, "Sex Composition and Corresponding Culture Patterns of Colonial America," *William and Mary Quarterly* (April, 1945), pp. 113–153; and Elizabeth Cometti, "Women in the American Revolution," *New England Quarterly* (September, 1947), pp. 329–346. Two books about women in the southern colonies are worthy of particular note: Julia C. Spruill, *Women's Life and Work in the Southern Colonies* (Chapel Hill, 1938); and Edmund S. Morgan, *Virginians at Home: Family Life in the Eighteenth Century* (Williamsburg, Va., 1952).

Women's involvement in benevolence and reform movements during the nineteenth century is well documented by such studies as Gerda Lerner, *The Grimké Sisters from South Carolina: Rebels Against Slavery* (Boston, 1967); Whitney R. Cross, *The Burned-Over District: The Social and Intellectual History of Enthusiastic Religion in Western New York, 1800–1850* (Ithaca, 1950); and Mary E. Massey, *Bonnet Brigades* (New York, 1966). In addition to the material already cited, which focuses on woman's status and the development of nineteenth-century social ideas that shaped her societal role, consult: Elizabeth A. Dexter, *Career Women of America, 1776–1840* (Francestown, N.H., 1950); John B. Blake, "Women and Medicine in Ante-Bellum America," *Bulletin of the History of Medicine* 39 (1965): 99–123; and Gail Parker, "Mary Baker Eddy and Sentimental Womanhood," *New England Quarterly* (March, 1970), pp. 3–18.

The woman-suffrage movement and American feminism have received some attention from historians. Biographies of such women as Lucretia Mott, Lucy Stone, Elizabeth Cady Stanton, Susan B. Anthony and Carrie Chapman Catt are numerous. While Eleanor Flexner's *Century of Struggle: the Woman's Rights Movement in the United States* (Cambridge, Mass., 1959) traces the movement's history with some success, there is no substitute for reading the *History of Woman Suffrage,* 6 vols. (New York and Rochester, 1881–1922), written and edited by the women who made the history (E. C. Stanton, S. B. Anthony, Ida H. Harper and Matilda J. Gage). Interpretive works are more scarce; the two best books remain Aileen S. Kraditor's *The Ideas of the Woman Suffrage Movement, 1890–1920* (New York, 1965); and William L. O'Neill's *Everyone Was Brave: The Rise and Fall of Feminism in America* (Chicago, 1969). Robert E. Riegel has formulated an interesting hypothesis regarding "Women's Clothes and Women's Rights," *American Quarterly* (Fall, 1963), pp. 390–401; while James M. McPherson's article "Abolitionists, Woman Suffrage, and the Negro, 1865–69," *Mid America* (January, 1965), pp. 40–47, is suggestive for understanding the underlying causes for the schism of 1869 in the woman-suffrage movement. A fine historical selection of feminist writings is edited by Wendy Martin, *The American Sister-*

hood: Writings of the Feminist Movement from Colonial Times to the Present (New York, 1972).

In addition to the essays by McGovern and Lasch there are impressive writings about women during the Progressive era and the 1920s that include Egal Feldman's "Prostitution, the Alien Woman and the Progressive Imagination, 1910–1915," *American Quarterly* (Summer, 1967), pp. 192–206; William O'Neill's *Divorce in the Progressive Era* (New Haven, 1967); and Anne F. Scott's "After Suffrage: Southern Women in the Twenties," *Journal of Southern History* (August, 1964), pp. 298–318. Noteworthy for tracing the development of larger themes that continue into the present century are Robert E. Riegel, "Changing American Attitudes toward Prostitution (1800–1920)," *Journal of the History of Ideas* (July-September, 1968), pp. 437–452; Thomas Woody, *A History of Women's Education in the United States,* 2 vols. (New York, 1929); Robert W. Smuts, *Women and Work in America* (New York, 1959), especially Chapter 4, "Women, Men and Work: Values and Attitudes," pp. 110–155; and Leo Kanowitz, *Women and the Law: the Unfinished Revolution* (Albuquerque, N.M., 1969).

With the exception of William H. Chafe's *The American Woman: Her Changing Social, Economic, and Political Roles, 1920–1970* (New York, 1972), and Stanley J. Lemons' *The Woman Citizen: Social Feminism in the 1920s* (Urbana, 1972), there are almost no available monographs that focus on the history of the American woman since the 1920s, although they do exist in unpublished form. The popular works of Vance Packard, Betty Friedan, Margaret Mead, Caroline Bird and Kate Millet, among others, are of limited value. Better use can be made of such studies as *American Women, the Report of the President's Commission on the Status of Women* (New York, 1965), edited by Margaret Mead and Frances B. Kaplan; and *Handbook on Women Workers,* Women's Bureau, Department of Labor (Washington, D.C., 1965) in tracing the plight of the modern-day woman. Probably the most imaginative analysis of past and present relationships between the sexes, black and white, has been done by black writers: Eldridge Cleaver, *Soul on Ice* (New York, 1968), "The Primeval Mitosis," 176–90; Calvin C. Hernton, *Sex and Racism in America* (New York, 1965); and William H. Grier and Price M. Cobbs, *Black Rage* (New York, 1968), Chapters 3–5.

1 2 3 4 5 6 7 8 9 10